HOW TO PASS

HIGHER
MUSIC

Joe McGowan

HODDER
GIBSON
AN HACHETTE UK COMPANY

Orders: please contact Bookpoint Ltd, 130 Milton Park, Abingdon, Oxon OX14 4SB. Telephone: (44) 01235 827720. Fax: (44) 01235 400454. Lines are open 9.00–5.00, Monday to Saturday, with a 24-hour message answering service. Visit our website at www.hoddereducation.co.uk. Hodder Gibson can be contacted direct on: Tel: 0141 848 1609; Fax: 0141 889 6315; email: hoddergibson@hodder.co.uk

© Joe McGowan 2006
First published in 2006 by
Hodder Gibson, an imprint of Hodder Education,
an Hachette UK company
2a Christie Street
Paisley PA1 1NB

Impression number   10 9 8 7 6 5 4 3
Year   2010   2009

Cover photo Rob Bartee / Alamy
Typeset in 9.5 on 12.5pt Frutiger Light by Phoenix Photosetting, Chatham, Kent
Printed and bound in Great Britain by Martins The Printers, Berwick-upon-Tweed

A catalogue record for this title is available from the British Library

ISBN-13: 978 0340 915 837

CONTENTS

Acknowledgements

Thanks to Peter Inness, Caroline Cochrane and the library staff at the Royal Scottish Academy of Music and Drama, Janet Young (Stonelaw High School), Alan MacLean, Simon Woolcott and everyone at Hodder Gibson, especially Elizabeth Hayes, my editor.

The Publishers would like to thank the following for permission to reproduce copyright material:

Track 1: Leggiadre ninfe, P. de Monte (The Amaryllis Consort). By kind permission of Pickwick Group Limited; Track 4: Exsultate Deo, Palestrina (Christ Church Cathedral Choir, director Stephen Darlington). By permission of Nimbus Records Ltd; Track 5: Kyrie (mass for Pentecost), Palestrina (Christ Church Cathedral Choir, director Stephen Darlington). By permission of Nimbus Records Ltd; Track 6: Concerto Grosso in F, Opus 6 No:2: 2. Allegro, performed by Trevor Pinnock, courtesy of Deutsche Grammophon, Part of the Universal Music Group; Track 7: The Creation H.21 No. 2: Mit Staunen Sieht Das Wundwerk…Und Laut Ertont Aus Ihren Kehlen, performed by John Eliot Gardiner, courtesy of Deutsche Grammophon, Part of the Universal Music Group; Track 8: 4. Recitativo: 'Ich steche fertig und bereit' Ich will den kreuzstab gerne tragen cantata, Bwv 56), performed by Thomas Quasthoff, courtesy of Deutsche Grammophon, Part of the Universal Music Group; Track 9: The Art of Fugue Bwv 1080: Contrapunctus 5, performed by Karl Munchinger, courtesy of The Decca Music Group, Part of the Universal Music Group; Track 10: Schwanengesang D975: No.4 Standchen, performed by Peter Schreier, courtesy of The Decca Music Group, Part of the Universal Music Group; Track 11: Don Giovanni K527: Non Mi Dir (Act 2), performed by Hakan Hagegard, courtesy of The Decca Music Group, Part of the Universal Music Group; Track 12: Symphony No. 4 in E Flat 'Romantic' 1. Bewegt, nicht zu schnell, performed Berliner Philharmoniker, courtesy of Deutsche Grammophon, Part of the Universal Music Group; Track 13: Symphony No. 9 D: 2. Im Tempo Eines Gemachlichen Landlers, performed by Georg Solti, courtesy of The Decca Music Group, Part of the Universal Music Group; Track 14: Lil Darlin, © Martin Taylor. By permission of P3 Music Ltd; Track 15: Schoenberg: Moses und Aron – Original version / Act 2 – Dieses Bild Bezeugt, performed by Pierre Boulez, courtesy of Deutsche Grammophon, Part of the Universal Music Group; Track 16: SOS, performed by ABBA, courtesy of Polydor Int'l, Part of the Universal Music Group; Track 17: 4. Rhythmique, performed by Wiener Philharmoniker, courtesy of Deutsche Grammophon, Part of the Universal Music Group; Track 27: Symphony No. 4 in E Flat 'Romantic' 2. Andante quasi Allegretto, performed by Berliner Philharmoniker, courtesy of Deutsche Grammophon, Part of the Universal Music Group; Track 28: Symphony No. 4 in E Flat 'Romantic' 1. Bewegt, nicht zu schnell, performed Berliner Philharmoniker, courtesy of Deutsche Grammophon, Part of the Universal Music Group; Track 29: Symphony No.8 in F Opus 93: 3. Tempo De Minuetto, performed by Claudio Abbado, courtesy of Deutsche Grammophon, Part of the Universal Music Group; Track 31: Symphonie Fantastique Opus 14: 3. Scene Aux Champs, performed by Georg Solti, courtesy of The Decca Music Group, Part of the Universal Music Group; Track 32: Sio Esca Vivo, O. de Lassus (The Amaryllis Consort). By kind permission of Pickwick Group Limited. Track 33: Symphony No.7 in A Opus 92:1 Poco Sostenuto – Vivace, performed by Wiener Philharmoniker, courtesy of Deutsche Grammophon, Part of the Universal Music Group; Track 34: Vivaldi: Oboe Concerto in C R.450 – 3. Allegro, performed by The Chamber Orchestra of Europe, courtesy of Deutsche Grammophon, Part of the Universal Music Group; Track 35: Porgy and Bess: Act 1: Headin' For the Promis' Lan', performed by Lorin Maazel, courtesy of The Decca Music Group, Part of the Universal Music Group; Track 36: Mozart: Le Nozze Di Figaro K.492 – Original Version, Vienna 178 – Se A Caso Madama – Or Bene, Ascolta, E Taci, performed by Georg Solti, courtesy of The Decca Music Group, Part of the Universal Music Group; Track 37: Jenufa: Jak Razem Vsecko To Stevkovo Vypin Ni Schl Plo, performed by Wiener Philharmoniker, courtesy of The Decca Music Group, Part of the Universal Music Group. Tracks 18–26 and 39–70: © Joe McGowan.

Every effort has been made to trace all copyright holders, but if any have been inadvertently overlooked the Publishers will be pleased to make the necessary arrangements at the first opportunity.

INTRODUCTION

Welcome!

Let me begin by congratulating you on reaching the standard of Higher Music, which is an achievement in itself.

If you have used a *How To Pass* book in music at a lower grade (or indeed any title in the *How To Pass* series) you will already be familiar with how things work: these books give you lots of exercises, tips and advice on all the stuff you need to know for your course assessments and exams. Our job is to *offer* all the help we can by making sure you know exactly what is involved in your course and have plenty of practice material to help you pass; your job is simply to *accept* that help by working through all that is being offered to you.

Although a revision guide book, *How To Pass Higher Music* can be used from the very start of your course to develop Listening, Composing and Arranging skills, so you are getting a two-for-one deal here – at no extra charge!

But enough babbling. The only things you need to know about *How To Pass Higher Music* for the moment can be summed up in four short points:

1 Work through this book carefully during your course to improve your skills.

2 Keep it handy for reference.

3 Use it for that all-important final revision.

4 Grow confident in the knowledge that you know *How To Pass*.

Good luck to you all!

THE HIGHER MUSIC QUALIFICATION

Higher Music gives you the opportunity to extend and develop the knowledge and skills you have acquired from previous grades. As in the earlier grades, the three main areas of musical activity are **Listening**, **Composing/Arranging** and **Performing**, but you have a number of options within these areas to cater for your personal musical interests and abilities.

Listening

Compulsory to all candidates (see also Chapters 1 and 2, pages 7–29)

Assessment

◆ Music question paper of one hour's duration (externally marked) *40 marks*

During your course you will learn a range of new musical concepts which will be heard in practice in a selection of reference works which you will study. The reference works will vary from year to year, but the musical concepts will remain the same. In May of the exam year you will sit a one hour Listening test based on these new concepts (and those from previous grades) and musical literacy (see Chapters 1 and 2). The excerpts used in this Listening test may include examples from the course reference works.

Composing/Arranging

(See also Chapter 4, page 41)

Assessment

◆ Folio of compositions/arrangements lasting a minimum of two minutes, including **two** examples of completed individual work

Composing/arranging will be assessed by your class teacher (and perhaps also an external assessor) and you will either be awarded a pass or a fail. Whilst the composing section does not contribute to your overall grade, **you must pass it** to be awarded your Higher Music qualification.

Performing or Performing with Technology

(See also Chapter 3, page 30)

There is an option for students to choose either a **Performing** or **Performing with Technology** route in their course.

Assessment – Performing

Students who choose the **Performing** route have two choices (each choice is worth 60 marks).

Choice 1   Either:

1   Perform a programme of prepared music lasting *ten minutes* and containing at least *two contrasting pieces* which are played *solo* and/or in a *group* on **one instrument** (which can be voice)

And

2   Perform a programme of prepared music lasting *five minutes* and containing at least *two contrasting pieces* which are played *solo* and/or in a *group* on a **different instrument**.

Choice 2   Or:

1   Perform a programme of prepared music lasting *ten minutes* and containing at least *two contrasting pieces* which are played *solo* and/or in a *group* on **one instrument** (which can be voice)

And

2   Perform a programme of prepared instrumental and/or vocal **accompaniments** lasting *eight minutes* and containing at least *two contrasting accompaniments*

And

3   Perform *at sight* **accompaniments** lasting a total of *two minutes* while the assessor plays the melody to be accompanied. Candidates will be allowed about five minutes to practise these accompaniments before the actual performance, and the assessor will indicate the *tempo* of each accompaniment.

Note: programmes may be performed on a single occasion or a number of separate occasions.

Assessment – Performing with Technology

Students who choose the **Performing with Technology** route have two choices (each choice is worth 60 marks).

Choice 1   Either:

1   Perform a programme of prepared music lasting *five minutes* and containing at least *two contrasting pieces* which are played *solo* and/or in a *group* on **one instrument** (which can be voice). The programme may be performed on a single occasion or a number of separate occasions.

And

2   Create a composition (or folio of compositions) or arrangement lasting at least three minutes using a MIDI sequencer

And

3   Take a Knowledge and Understanding Test (lasting around 45 minutes) based on MIDI sequencing concepts/techniques.

Choice 2   Or:

1   Perform a programme of prepared music lasting *five minutes* and containing at least *two contrasting pieces* which are played *solo* and/or in a *group* on **one instrument** (which can be voice). The programme may be performed on a single occasion or a number of separate occasions.

And

2   Produce a stereo master recording of at least *two* pieces of music using Sound Engineering and Production techniques

And

3   Take a Knowledge and Understanding Test (lasting around 45 minutes) based on Sound Engineering and Production concepts/techniques.

Students will be required to achieve a number of Learning Outcomes and undertake various performance criteria in the Performing with Technology route; these will be assessed in the above tasks and in the form of observation checklists carried out by the teacher.

HOW TO USE THIS BOOK

There is no particular order in which you should work through this book, since all of the material is linked together by the common aspects of musical concepts, techniques and features which are relevant to every part of the Higher Music course.

Chapters 1 and **2** deal specifically with Listening skills, and in particular with the mandatory Listening test question paper which you will take in May of the exam year, but the areas of knowledge required for these chapters will also assist you in your composing and/or arranging projects.

Chapter 3 relates to Performing and Performing with Technology, and contains glossaries of terms and concepts used in MIDI Sequencing and Sound Engineering and Production which will be especially useful to those who select either of these options.

Chapter 4 consists of four workshops in which you are guided step-by-step through the composing and arranging processes involved in creating four contrasting pieces of music, with the opportunity to compose your own piece in the same styles as those used in each workshop.

'For Practice' exercises

The purpose of these exercises is to present you with tasks and exercises which allow you to put into practice many of the techniques and concepts you will encounter through the book, as well as ensure that you understand the material you are working on.

'Hints and Tips'

These are little snippets of information which pop up here and there to give you some helpful advice and facts on specific topics along the way.

CD-based exercises and examples

This book comes with a CD containing musical excerpts and examples for use with Chapters 1, 2 and 4. The particular track that you need to listen to in relation to a question or exercise will be clearly indicated in the text.

Glossary of Higher Music Concepts

Definitions of the musical concepts introduced in Higher Music can be found in the Glossary, page 121. A knowledge of musical concepts introduced in earlier grades will be assumed, but a summary of these is also listed in the Glossary.

Note: musical concepts appear in **bold** type throughout the book.

Useful websites

◆ **www.ltscotland.org.uk**
Learning and Teaching Scotland. Free downloads and information on music courses from Access 3 to Advanced Higher level.

◆ **www.sqa.org.uk**
The Scottish Qualifications Authority. Up-to-date information on music courses and exam arrangements, with some free downloads available.

◆ **www.liberton.edin.sch.uk**
Liberton High School. Information and audio samples relating to musical concepts studied at all levels.

◆ **www.bbc.co.uk/schools/gcsebitesize**
The BBC's schools 'bitesize' website. Although dedicated to GCSE qualifications, this website contains information and audio samples which will be helpful to students studying Scottish curriculum music courses.

◆ **www.abrsm.org**
The Associated Board of the Royal Schools of Music, 24 Portland Place, London W1B 1LU. Tel: 020 7636 5400   E-mail: abrsm@abrsm.ac.uk   A range of publications relating to graded music exams (including free syllabuses giving details of suitable pieces for different instruments at each grade) and music theory are available from this source.

◆ **www.trinitycollege.co.uk**
Guildhall School of Music & Drama. Trinity Guildhall Examinations, 89 Albert Embankment, London SE1 7TP, UK. Tel: 020 7820 6100.
E-mail: trinityguildhall@trinitycollege.co.uk   This is a useful source for a range of publications relating to graded music exams (including free syllabuses giving details of suitable pieces for different instruments at each grade).

◆ **www.tvuapac.com**
Rockschool, London College of Music. LCM Examinations, Thames Valley University, Walpole House, 18–22 Bond Street, London W5 5AA. Tel: 020 8231 2364.
E-mail: lcm.exams@tvu.ac.uk   Another useful source for publications and information relating to graded music exams (including free syllabuses giving details of suitable pieces for different instruments at each grade).

◆ **www.rockschool.co.uk**
Rockschool. 245 Sandycombe Road, Kew, Richmond, Surrey, TW9 2EW. Tel: 020 8332 6303.   E-mail: sandie@rockschool.co.uk   Publications and information relating to the *Rock School* graded rock/pop exams (these exams focus on vocals, guitar, bass guitar, piano/keyboard and drums).

◆ **www.karadar.com**
Classical music dictionary. Composer biographies and their music, photos, MIDI and MP3 downloads.

Chapter 1

REVISING HIGHER MUSIC CONCEPTS

This chapter is based on Listening exercises which will help you to revise the new musical concepts studied at Higher level, but you will also need to have a good knowledge of concepts learnt in earlier grades, as the exercises cover a wide range of music.

Refer to the Glossary (page 121) for definitions of Higher Music concepts as well as a full list of concepts from previous grades which you may need to review before working through this chapter. For definitions and exercises relating to concepts from previous grades, see *How To Pass Standard Grade Music*.

For Practice

◆ Listening to different kinds of music is the only way to become better at identifying concepts by ear. When you have worked through the exercises in this chapter, select recordings of music in a wide variety of musical styles from the early medieval and renaissance periods right up to the present day, and listen carefully to identify as many concepts and features as you can which are present in the various recordings.

◆ A good way to sharpen your listening skills is to practise making notes about what you hear every time you listen to a piece of music. Start by listening for obvious features like **structure**, **tonality**, **metre** and **style**, then, during the second listening, try to pick out details like individual instruments, **dynamics**, **melodic** features (**ornaments**, **staccato**, **legato**, etc.) and **texture**. The more you practise this, the quicker you will become at identifying the important features in any kind of music.

◆ For you and your fellow students to test yourselves, why not choose recordings and set your own tests for each other using the exercises in this chapter as a guide? It's more interesting that way, and great practice for Listening tests!

Hints and Tips

When you have to identify, from a list, a number of concepts present in a musical excerpt (in Listening test question papers, for example), rather than try to listen for *specific* concepts from the list during the first listening, you may find it helpful to make a quick note of the *obvious* features you hear in the music, then compare this with the options on the question paper. Any features from your notes which match those on the question paper will probably be correct answers. Another method is to begin by eliminating from the list those features which you think are definitely *not* present, leaving you with a shorter list of possible correct answers.

Hints and Tips

Certain musical forms sometimes have features in common which can make it a little difficult to tell them apart by ear. The **Motet**, **Mass**, **Passion**, **Anthem** and **Oratorio**, for example, are all religious vocal works which present such a challenge.

A good way to approach this identification problem is, rather than allow yourself to be distracted by the *similarities* between such musical forms/structures, make sure you understand and can identify the features which *separate* one from another. For instance, in an **Oratorio** you will be expecting to hear an **orchestra** and **choruses**, and perhaps also **soloists**, so the whole structure is generally 'bigger' and less solemn than other religious vocal music.

The **Mass**, on the other hand, has clearly defined sections such as the *Kyrie, Gloria, Credo,* and *Sanctus Benedictus* (see Glossary, page 121), the Latin titles of which are actually sung, so if you hear the word 'Kyrie' or 'Credo' being sung then the excerpt you are listening to almost certainly comes from a Mass. This simple characteristic feature is sufficient to separate the Mass from most other similar-sounding works. Similarly, the *absence* of such key words would normally eliminate the possibility of the work being a Mass.

You can therefore identify the style or form of a piece of music not only by picking out what you hear but also by eliminating what you do not hear.

For Practice

A great way to become efficient at identifying the unique or characteristic features of various musical styles/forms is to make a short bullet-point list of these features and then listen to several examples of each until you gradually improve your ability to recognise them by ear. By doing this you will become confident in knowing which characteristic features are present in a musical excerpt and which aren't.

The following Listening exercises have been placed into six broad categories to help you focus on and revise specific musical periods, concepts and aspects of the course. Note that certain concepts, although listed under a particular category, may be found in music from several different periods (for example, *Tierce de Picardie* is common in music of both the renaissance and baroque periods).

Section 1: Concepts associated with early music

In this section, many of the musical concepts you need to know about are associated with the **medieval** and **renaissance** periods. Before attempting the following exercises, make sure you fully understand the meaning of each of the Higher Music concepts at the top of the following page, and are confident in your ability to recognise them by ear. You might also find it helpful to jot down a little information about each concept – e.g. its characteristic features – to jog your memory before you begin.

- renaissance
- pavan
- galliard
- mode
- hemiola
- antiphonal
- air
- hymn tune

- tierce de Picardie
- ballett
- madrigal
- mass
- consort
- anthem
- motet
- chant

Listening Exercise 1: CD Track 1

Read the question and the features below very carefully before listening to CD track 1. Try to answer the question after hearing the recorded excerpt no more than **twice**.

Question 1. Listen to CD track1 and tick **one** box in **Column One** to describe the form/structure and **one** box in **Column Two** to describe a feature present.

Column One	Column Two
☐ Motet	☐ Sprechgesang
☐ Madrigal	☐ Hemiola
☐ Pavan	☐ Homophony
☐ Anthem	☐ Syncopation

Listening Exercise 2: CD Track 2

Read the question and the features below very carefully before listening to CD track 2. Try to answer the question after hearing the recorded excerpt no more than **twice**.

Question 2. Listen to CD track 2 and tick **one** box in **Column One** to describe the form/structure and **one** box in **Column Two** to describe a feature present.

Column One	Column Two
☐ Ballett	☐ Voices in harmony
☐ Mass	☐ Polyphony
☐ Chant	☐ Voices in unison
☐ Antiphonal	☐ Descant

Listening Exercise 3: CD Track 3

Read the question and the features below very carefully before listening to CD track 3. Try to answer the question after hearing the recorded excerpt no more than **twice**.

Question 3. Listen to CD track 3 and tick **one** box in **Column One** to describe the form/structure and **one** box in **Column Two** to describe a feature present.

Column One	Column Two
☐ Galliard	☐ Ground bass
☐ Air	☐ Glissando
☐ Pavan	☐ Triple metre
☐ Ballett	☐ Alberti bass

Listening Exercise 4: CD Track 4

Read the question and the features below very carefully before listening to CD track 4. Try to answer the question after hearing the recorded excerpt no more than **twice**.

Question 4. Listen to CD track 4 and tick **one** box in **Column One** to describe the form/structure and **one** box in **Column Two** to describe a feature present.

Column One	Column Two
☐ Motet	☐ Triple metre
☐ Hymn tune	☐ Melismatic
☐ Chant	☐ Ritardando (*rit.*)
☐ Pavan	☐ Trill

Listening Exercise 5: CD Track 5

Read the question and the features below very carefully before listening to CD track 5. Try to answer the question after hearing the recorded excerpt no more than **twice**.

Question 5. Listen to CD track 5 and tick **one** box in **Column One** to describe the form/structure and **one** box in **Column Two** to describe a feature present.

Column One	Column Two
☐ Consort	☐ Hemiola
☐ Antiphonal	☐ Tierce de Picardie
☐ Madrigal	☐ Polyphonic
☐ Mass	☐ Strophic

Section 2: Concepts associated with baroque music

In this section many of the musical concepts you need to know about are associated with the **baroque** period. Before attempting the following exercises make sure you fully understand the meaning of each of the Higher Music concepts below, and are confident in your ability to recognise them by ear. (Remember that it might help to write down a little bit about each concept in order to jog your memory before you begin.)

- ripieno
- concertino
- concerto grosso
- oratorio
- chaconne/passacaglia
- fugue
- tonal answer
- real answer
- Da capo aria
- prelude
- basso continuo

- ritornello
- augmentation
- diminution
- cantata
- suite
- passion
- recitative
- chorale
- French overture
- Italian overture
- ornaments: acciaccatura; appoggiatura; mordent; turn; trill

Listening Exercise 6: CD Track 6

Read the question and the features which follow very carefully before listening to CD track 6. Try to answer the question after hearing the recorded excerpt no more than **twice**.

Question 6. Listen to CD track 6 and tick **three** boxes to describe what you hear.

☐ Concerto grosso

☐ Galliard

☐ Passion

☐ Pizzicato

☐ Turn

☐ Italian overture

☐ Imitation

☐ Ripieno

☐ Col legno

Listening Exercise 7: CD Track 7

Read the question and the features below very carefully before listening to CD track 7. Try to answer the question after hearing the recorded excerpt no more than **twice**.

Question 7. Listen to CD track 7 and tick **three** boxes to describe what you hear.

☐ Concertino

☐ Chorale

☐ Oratorio

☐ Cantata

☐ Homophonic SATB

☐ Da Capo aria

☐ Prelude

☐ Sequence

☐ Overture

Listening Exercise 8: CD Track 8

Read the question and the features below very carefully before listening to CD track 8. Try to answer the question after hearing the recorded excerpt no more than **twice**.

Question 8. Listen to CD track 8 and tick **three** boxes to describe what you hear.

☐ Chorale

☐ Melismatic

☐ Cantata

☐ Trill

☐ A cappella

☐ Syllabic

☐ Ritornello

☐ Sequence

☐ Pedal

Listening Exercise 9: CD Track 9

Read the question and the features which follow very carefully before listening to CD track 9. Try to answer the question after hearing the recorded excerpt no more than **twice**.

Question 9. Listen to CD track 9 and tick **three** boxes to describe what you hear.

☐ French overture

☐ Fugue

☐ Suite

☐ Real Answer

☐ Through-composed

☐ Basso continuo

☐ Legato

☐ Mordent

☐ Augmentation

Section 3: Concepts associated with classical and romantic music

In this section many of the musical concepts you need to know about are associated with the **classical** and **romantic** periods. Before attempting the following exercises make sure you fully understand the meaning of each of the Higher Music concepts below, and are confident in your ability to recognise them by ear. (Remember that it might help to write down a little bit about each concept in order to jog your memory before you begin.)

- nationalist
- late romantic
- tonal sequence
- scherzo
- consonance
- dissonance
- three against two
- ballet
- chorus
- harmonic and melodic minor

- Leitmotiv
- stretto
- sonata form
- symphonic/tone poem
- song cycle
- Lied
- transition
- bridge
- exposition
- coloratura

Listening Exercise 10: CD Track 10
Read the question and the features below very carefully before listening to CD track 10. Try to answer the question after hearing the recorded excerpt no more than **three times**.

Question 10. Listen to CD track 10 and tick **four** boxes to describe what you hear.

☐ Symphonic/tone poem

☐ Lied

☐ Scherzo

☐ Triplets

☐ Note clusters

☐ Harmonic minor

☐ Staccato

☐ Exposition

☐ Dissonance

☐ Stretto

Listening Exercise 11: CD Track 11

Read the question and the features below very carefully before listening to CD track 11. Try to answer the question after hearing the recorded excerpt no more than **three times**.

Question 11. Listen to CD track 11 and tick **four** boxes to describe what you hear.

☐ Melodic minor

☐ Coloratura

☐ Stretto

☐ Exposition

☐ Cantata

☐ Nationalist

☐ Appoggiatura

☐ Aria

☐ Leitmotiv

☐ Opera

Listening Exercise 12: CD Track 12

Read the question and the features below very carefully before listening to CD track 12. Try to answer the question after hearing the recorded excerpt no more than **three times**.

Question 12. Listen to CD track 12 and tick **four** boxes to describe what you hear.

☐ Classical

☐ Romantic

☐ Tremolando/tremolo

☐ Atonal

☐ Accelerando

☐ Three against two

☐ Concerto

☐ Symphony

☐ Mode

☐ Compound time

Listening Exercise 13: CD Track 13

Read the question and the features below very carefully before listening to CD track 13. Try to answer the question after hearing the recorded excerpt no more than **three times**.

Question 13. Listen to CD track 13 and tick **four** boxes to describe what you hear.

☐ Acciaccatura

☐ Ostinato

☐ Muted trumpets

☐ Inverted pedal

☐ Cadenza

☐ Late romantic

☐ Musique concrète

☐ Suspension

☐ Flutter-tonguing

☐ Ritardando (*rit.*)

Section 4: Concepts associated with modern music

In this section many of the musical concepts you need to know about are associated with **modern music**. Before attempting the following exercises make sure you fully understand the meaning of each of the Higher Music concepts below, and are confident in your ability to recognise them by ear. (Remember that it might help to write down a little bit about each concept in order to jog your memory before you begin.)

◆ microtone

◆ tritone

◆ tone row

◆ inversion

◆ organised sound

◆ retrograde

◆ bridge

◆ jazz-funk

◆ heterophony

◆ time changes

◆ harmonics

◆ serial

◆ polytonality

◆ irregular metres

Listening Exercise 14: CD Track 14

Read the question and the features below very carefully before listening to CD track 14. Try to answer the question after hearing the recorded excerpt no more than **three times**.

Question 14. Listen to CD track 14 and tick **four** boxes to describe what you hear.

☐ Trill

☐ Tone row

☐ Organised sound

☐ Double stopping

☐ Distortion

☐ Harmonics

☐ Heterophony

☐ Glissando

☐ Tritone

☐ Harmonic minor

Listening Exercise 15: CD Track 15

Read the question and the features which follow very carefully before listening to CD track 15. Try to answer the question after hearing the recorded excerpt no more than **three times**.

Question 15. Listen to CD track 15 and tick **four** boxes to describe what you hear.

- ☐ Bridge
- ☐ Serial
- ☐ Organised sound
- ☐ Pizzicato
- ☐ Cross rhythms
- ☐ Harmonics
- ☐ Heterophony
- ☐ Glissando
- ☐ Reverb

Listening Exercise 16: CD Track 16

Read the question and the features below very carefully before listening to CD track 16. Try to answer the question after hearing the recorded excerpt no more than **three times**.

Question 16. Listen to CD track 16 and tick **four** boxes to describe what you hear.

- ☐ Modulation
- ☐ Rubato
- ☐ Sequence
- ☐ Retrograde
- ☐ Reverb
- ☐ Time changes
- ☐ Bridge
- ☐ Jazz-funk
- ☐ Polytonality
- ☐ Soul music

Listening Exercise 17: CD Track 17

Read the question and the features below very carefully before listening to CD track 17. Try to answer the question after hearing the recorded excerpt no more than **three times**.

Question 17. Listen to CD track 17 and tick **four** boxes to describe what you hear.

- ☐ Jazz-funk
- ☐ Pitched percussion
- ☐ Irregular metres
- ☐ Concerto
- ☐ Unpitched percussion
- ☐ Whole-tone scale
- ☐ Tone Row
- ☐ Neo-classical
- ☐ Musique concrète
- ☐ Minimalist

HOW TO PASS HIGHER MUSIC

Section 5: Chords and cadences

In this section you will revise **chords** and **cadences**. It is likely that you are already familiar with most of the cadences, but the chords are new to Higher Music, and as well as recognising these at sight from notation (you may be asked to do this in a test paper), you also need to be able to identify them by ear.

- ◆ dominant 7th chord
- ◆ major 7th chord
- ◆ diminished 7th chord
- ◆ augmented chord
- ◆ added 6th chord

- ◆ perfect cadence
- ◆ imperfect cadence
- ◆ plagal cadence
- ◆ interrupted cadence

For Practice

Before attempting this section you should fully understand how each chord and cadence is constructed, and play them several times until you can confidently recognise their characteristic sounds. To begin with, try playing the various chords and cadences on a harmonic instrument such as the piano or a keyboard to familiarise yourself with the unique sound of each, then get a fellow student to test you by playing them at random to see how many you can recognise. For information on the chords used in this exercise, see the Glossary, page 121.

Hints and Tips

Since each of the chords and cadences you need to be able to recognise by ear has a particular sound, it is possible to make mental notes which will help you to identify them. For example, you could keep a memory-file like this in your head:

Perfect cadence – an ending; *closes* a phrase

Imperfect cadence – more music to come; keeps the phrase *open*

Plagal cadence – sounds like 'Amen' at the end of a hymn; closes a phrase

Interrupted cadence – sounds as though it's leading to a perfect cadence but ends on a chord which creates a 'surprise' by keeping the phrase open or unfinished

Added 6th chord – has a mellow sound where you can hear the effect of the added 6th note creating a cool, relaxed, 'jazzy' mood

Diminished 7th chord – rather discordant, strong sound… a bit scary!

Dominant 7th chord – like the dominant chord with an extra 'edge' to it – this 'edge' being the added 7th note which makes the chord sound a bit more forceful than the plain dominant chord

Hints and *Tips continued* ➤

Hints and *Tips* continued

Major 7th chord – has a distinctive warm, dreamy, 'floating' sound (good for creating a sense of open space or of soaring high in the sky); also a 'jazzy' sound

Augmented chord – sounds like the music 'lifts' rather like an imperfect cadence, keeping the phrase open; a strong sounding chord, not as 'mellow' as the 6th, dominant 7th or major 7th

Don't worry if identifying chords seems difficult (if not impossible!) at first. As in other areas of Listening, you need gradually to train your ear to recognise their specific sounds, and the best way to do that is to keep *playing* them, keep *listening* to all kinds of music, and keep *testing* yourself on a regular basis.

The following exercises require you to listen to various chords and cadences and identify them by ticking the appropriate box.

Note: In each of the following four **cadence** tracks (tracks 18–21) you will hear a progression of chords, the last *two* of which form the cadence you have to identify.

Listening Exercise 18: CD Track 18
Question 18. Listen to CD track 18 and tick **one** box to describe the type of **cadence** you hear.

☐ Perfect

☐ Imperfect

☐ Plagal

☐ Interrupted

Listening Exercise 19: CD Track 19
Question 19. Listen to CD track 19 and tick **one** box to describe the type of **cadence** you hear.

☐ Perfect

☐ Imperfect

☐ Plagal

☐ Interrupted

Listening Exercise 20: CD Track 20
Question 20. Listen to CD track 20 and tick **one** box to describe the type of **cadence** you hear.

☐ Perfect

☐ Imperfect

☐ Plagal

☐ Interrupted

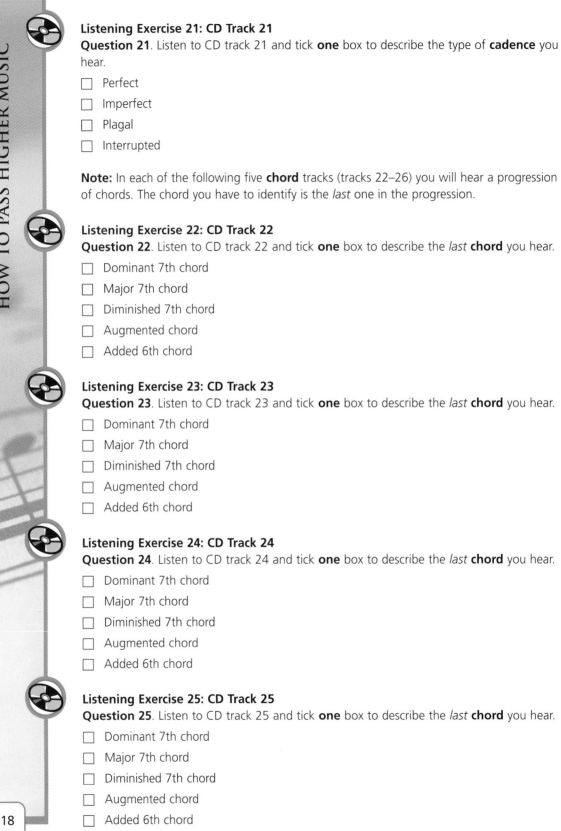

Listening Exercise 21: CD Track 21

Question 21. Listen to CD track 21 and tick **one** box to describe the type of **cadence** you hear.

☐ Perfect

☐ Imperfect

☐ Plagal

☐ Interrupted

Note: In each of the following five **chord** tracks (tracks 22–26) you will hear a progression of chords. The chord you have to identify is the *last* one in the progression.

Listening Exercise 22: CD Track 22

Question 22. Listen to CD track 22 and tick **one** box to describe the *last* **chord** you hear.

☐ Dominant 7th chord

☐ Major 7th chord

☐ Diminished 7th chord

☐ Augmented chord

☐ Added 6th chord

Listening Exercise 23: CD Track 23

Question 23. Listen to CD track 23 and tick **one** box to describe the *last* **chord** you hear.

☐ Dominant 7th chord

☐ Major 7th chord

☐ Diminished 7th chord

☐ Augmented chord

☐ Added 6th chord

Listening Exercise 24: CD Track 24

Question 24. Listen to CD track 24 and tick **one** box to describe the *last* **chord** you hear.

☐ Dominant 7th chord

☐ Major 7th chord

☐ Diminished 7th chord

☐ Augmented chord

☐ Added 6th chord

Listening Exercise 25: CD Track 25

Question 25. Listen to CD track 25 and tick **one** box to describe the *last* **chord** you hear.

☐ Dominant 7th chord

☐ Major 7th chord

☐ Diminished 7th chord

☐ Augmented chord

☐ Added 6th chord

Listening Exercise 26: CD Track 26

Question 26. Listen to CD track 26 and tick **one** box to describe the *last* **chord** you hear.

☐ Dominant 7th chord

☐ Major 7th chord

☐ Diminished 7th chord

☐ Augmented chord

☐ Added 6th chord

Section 6: Musical literacy

In addition to knowledge of a wide range of musical concepts, the Higher Music course requires that you have a certain understanding of music notation; this is commonly referred to as music theory or musical literacy.

Part of your final written (or 'Listening') test paper will contain questions relating to this aspect, and you should therefore ensure that you are familiar with the rudiments of music notation.

Below is a list of the kinds of musical literacy tasks you need to be able to carry out.

On examining (at sight) the notation of a piece of music, you should be able to:

◆ describe the **interval** between two notes as a semitone, third, fifth, octave, etc.

◆ **transpose** part of a melody up or down an octave

◆ identify **chords**, **cadences**, **scales**, **ornaments** and musical symbols (including articulation marks such as **slurs**, **staccato** dots and **accents**)

◆ give the meaning of basic Italian terms (e.g. *Dal Segno*, *Da Capo*, *a tempo* etc.) which appear on the score

◆ identify and correct rhythmic errors and incorrect bars

◆ identify where the main beats and up-beats are.

Upon hearing the musical excerpt for which you have been given the music notation, you should also be able to:

◆ write any notes, rests and/or musical rhythms which are missing from a particular bar

◆ identify where certain events occur in the music – for example, where a specific instrument starts playing. You will normally do this by placing a cross (**X**) above the relevant note or bar

◆ insert missing **time signatures**

◆ identify any special features relating to musical concepts you have studied (for example, the **style** or **texture** of the excerpt).

There now follow three musical literacy exercises which are typical of the kind you can expect in your Listening test paper. (Question 4 of the sample Listening test paper on page 25 is another.)

Musical literacy Exercise 1

This question is based on a short orchestral excerpt. The music for the **flute** part in this excerpt is given. Study the music and the questions which follow before listening to the excerpt on CD track 27.

Musical Literacy Exercise 1: CD Track 27
Question 27. Listen to CD track 27 whilst following the music for the flute part printed below. Afterwards, try to answer the questions after hearing the track no more than a further **three times**.

(a) State the time signature

(b) Place a bracket ( ) over the *last* occurrence of two notes which are a **semitone** apart.

(c) Insert the rest omitted from bar 6.

(d) Name the concept which best describes a feature of the bass part.

_____

(e) Give the meaning of the lines _____ above the notes.

_____

(f) Give the meaning of _____ at bar 6.

_____

Musical literacy Exercise 2

This question is based on a short orchestral excerpt. The music for the **first violins** part in this excerpt is given. Study this music and the questions which follow before listening to the excerpt on CD track 28.

Musical Literacy Exercise 2: CD Track 28
Question 28. Listen to CD track 28 whilst following the music of the first violins part printed on the following page. Afterwards, try to answer the questions after hearing the track no more than a further **three times**.

(a) Give the meaning of the line  stretching between the notes in bars

1–2, bars 3–4, bars 9–10 and bars 11–12.

_____

(b) Re-write bars 5–8 **two octaves lower** in the bass clef.

(c) Place a bracket ([   ]) over the **first** occurrence of two notes which are an interval of a third apart.

(d) Write the number of the bar in which the rhythm is incorrectly printed.

_____

(e) Complete bar 11.

(f) Name the musical technique (concept) which begins at bar 9.

_____

Musical literacy Exercise 3

This question is based on a short orchestral excerpt. The music for the **first violins** part in this excerpt is given on the following page. Study this music and the questions which follow before listening to the excerpt on CD track 29.

Musical Literacy Exercise 3: CD Track 29

Question 29. Listen to CD track 29 whilst following the music of the first violins part printed below. Afterwards, try to answer the questions after hearing the track no more than a further **three times**.

(a) State the time signature.

(b) Give the meaning of **sf**. _____

(c) Place a cross (**X**) above the **note** where the timpani enter.

(d) Re-write bars 4–7 **one octave lower**.

(e) Place a box around a **passing note**.

(f) What do the lines ⌐1. ⌐2. above bars 11 and 12 mean?

_____

(g) What is the meaning of the sign ♮ beside the notes in bars 6 and 7?

_____

Chapter 2

SPECIMEN LISTENING TEST QUESTION PAPER

Question 1

(a) CD Track 30

This excerpt is based on classical guitar music. Read through the list of features below before listening to the music.

Tick **four** boxes to identify features present in the music. Try to complete your answers after hearing the excerpt no more than **three times**.

- ☐ Organised sound
- ☐ Rubato
- ☐ Riff
- ☐ Heterophony
- ☐ Tremolando/tremolo
- ☐ Syncopation
- ☐ Polytonality
- ☐ Broken chords
- ☐ Slurs
- ☐ Hemiola

(b) Listen to **CD track 30** again and answer questions (i) and (ii)

(i) Describe the tonality. _____

(ii) Tick **one** box to identify a feature present

- ☐ Delay
- ☐ Tone row
- ☐ Duet
- ☐ Double stopping

Question 2

CD Track 31

This excerpt comes from *Symphonie Fantastique* by Berlioz. A 'musical map' of the excerpt is laid out on the following page; read the question very carefully before listening to CD track 31. As you can see, you are required to insert information in six specific areas. A voice will guide you through the excerpt as you listen. Try to complete this question after listening to the excerpt no more **three times**.

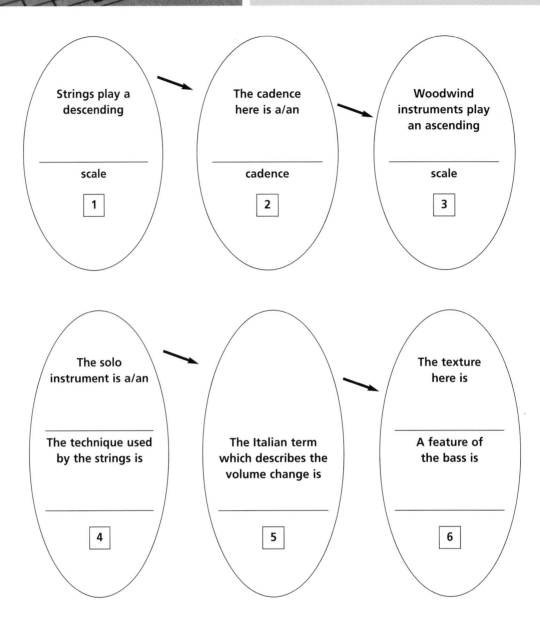

Strings play a descending _____ **scale** | 1

→

The cadence here is a/an _____ **cadence** | 2

→

Woodwind instruments play an ascending _____ **scale** | 3

The solo instrument is a/an _____ **The technique used by the strings is** _____ | 4

→

The Italian term which describes the volume change is _____ | 5

→

The texture here is _____ **A feature of the bass is** _____ | 6

Question 3

CD Track 32

This is an excerpt of vocal music. Read through the list of features below before listening to the music.

Tick **four** boxes to identify features present in the music. Try to complete your answers after hearing the excerpt no more than **three times**.

☐ Plainchant

☐ Chorale prelude

☐ Renaissance

☐ Homophony

☐ Consort

- ☐ Tierce de Picardie
- ☐ Lied
- ☐ Baroque
- ☐ Imitative polyphony
- ☐ Mass

Question 4

(a) CD Track 33

This question is based on orchestral music. Read through questions (i)–(vii) before listening to CD track 33. As you listen, follow the music for this excerpt which is printed below. Then, try to complete your answers to the questions after hearing the excerpt no more than a further **three** times.

(i) Name the ornament ♪ which appears throughout the excerpt.

_____

(ii) State the time signature. ☐

(iii) On which beats of the bar are the notes in bars 9–12 played?

_____

(iv) Name the ascending scale which occurs in this same section (bars 9–12).

_____

(v) Put a box around two notes which are an **octave** apart.

(vi) What does **cresc.** (bar 1) mean? _____

(vii) Give the meaning of the dots which appear **above** some of the notes in bars 2, 3 and 8, and bars 9–12. _____

(b) Listen to **CD track 33** again and tick **one** box in **Column One** to describe the style and **one** box in **Column Two** to describe the form/structure. Try to complete your answers after hearing the excerpt again no more than **once**.

Column One

☐ Baroque
☐ Classical
☐ Late romantic
☐ Minimalist

Column Two

☐ Consort
☐ Passacaglia
☐ Concerto
☐ Symphony

Question 5

(a) CD Track 34

This is an excerpt of instrumental music. Read through the list of features below before listening to the music.

Tick **three** boxes to identify features present in the music. Try to complete your answers after hearing the excerpt no more than **twice**.

☐ Dissonance
☐ Baroque
☐ Galliard
☐ Basso continuo
☐ Compound time
☐ Concerto
☐ French overture
☐ Scherzo

(b) Listen to the excerpt again, then answer questions (i) and (ii).

(i) Name the **solo** instrument playing. _____

(ii) Tick **two** boxes to describe features present in the **solo** part.

☐ Syncopation
☐ Sequence
☐ Flutter-tonguing
☐ Ostinato
☐ Pedal
☐ Staccato
☐ Interrupted cadence
☐ Microtone

Question 6

CD Track 35. In this question you are asked to describe the music you hear by inserting the appropriate concepts and features in the text on the following page. Read through the question carefully before listening to CD track 35, and aim to complete the exercise after hearing the recorded excerpt no more than **three times**.

The excerpt begins with the vocal line 'Oh I got my ticket ready and the time is gettin' short 'cos we're leavin' today…' The type (range) of voice singing this line is a _____. The solo voice is soon accompanied by a _____ of singers. Shortly after this, the composer uses certain instruments/musical devices to suggest a moving train; list at least THREE of these:

_____

_____.

Music which describes something in this way is called _____.

A section then begins with the singers accompanied by solo piano. A word to describe the style of the singing here is _____, and a feature of the piano accompaniment is _____.

When the piano stops playing the singers begin an unaccompanied section; this kind of unaccompanied singing is known as _____, and the structure here is _____. From here to the end of the excerpt the voices sing the same lyrics but not in unison; the higher-pitched voices sing the melody in quicker note values than those at the lower pitch – this is known as _____, whereas the lower voices do the opposite and sing the notes in longer note values, which is known as _____.

Finally, what style or styles of music (i.e. folk, rock, blues, etc.) do you think had the greatest influence on the composition of this piece?_____

Question 7

CD Tracks 36 and 37. You will now compare two excerpts of vocal music. Listed in the **left** column of the answer pages which follow are a range of musical concepts. From that column you should select features which are present in the excerpts by placing a tick in the appropriate column (**EXCERPT 1, EXCERPT 2, COMMON TO BOTH EXCERPTS**). The maximum number of concepts you should select from each column is indicated at the bottom of [GRID 2] Final answer; you should not exceed that number of concepts.

Read the answer pages carefully before listening to CD tracks 36 and 37 and tick the musical concepts in each piece under the headings given in the appropriate column in **[GRID 1]. This is your rough work.**

After listening to each excerpt no more than **three times**, put your final answers in **[GRID 2]**.

[GRID 1]: Rough working only

CONCEPTS	EXCERPT 1	EXCERPT 2	COMMON TO BOTH EXCERPTS
MELODIC Trill			
Imitation			
Atonal			
Modal			
Microtone			
HARMONIC Suspension			
Modulation			
Polytonality			
Whole-tone scale			
Alberti bass			
STRUCTURAL Canon			
Ostinato			
Triple metre			
Aria			
Polyphonic			
STYLES/FORMS Baroque			
Classical			
Late romantic			
Opera			
Oratorio			

[GRID 2]: Final answer

CONCEPTS	EXCERPT 1	EXCERPT 2	COMMON TO BOTH EXCERPTS
MELODIC Trill			
Imitation			
Atonal			
Modal			
Microtone			
HARMONIC Suspension			
Modulation			
Polytonality			
Whole-tone scale			
Alberti bass			
STRUCTURAL Canon			
Ostinato			
Triple metre			
Aria			
Polyphonic			
STYLES/FORMS Baroque			
Classical			
Late romantic			
Opera			
Oratorio			
	2 marks	3 marks	3 marks

PERFORMING

The Higher Music course allows you several options in this area, with *Performing*, *Accompanying* and *Performing with Technology* all available to you (see **The Higher Music Qualification**, page 2).

If you select the Performing option you will give a live performance of pieces from your prepared programme (lasting at least 10 minutes) on one instrument (which can, of course, be voice), with the choice to perform either solo (for 5 minutes) or as an accompanist (for 8 minutes) on another instrument. If you choose the accompanying option, your assessment will include performing an accompaniment at sight.

Your performances may be undertaken on a single occasion or on a number of separate occasions, and your teacher and/or instrumental instructor (if you have one) will advise you on choosing a suitable programme of pieces for this assessment. Take note, however, that your programme has to contain at least *two* contrasting pieces and must be at least Grade 4 standard as set by the Associated Board of the Royal Schools of Music, Trinity Guildhall, Rock School, or London College of Music. For guidelines on pieces for your instrument(s) which meet this standard, see the examination syllabus booklets published by these centres; these are free and can be picked up from many music stores or ordered direct from the various music schools/colleges (contact/website details on page 6).

Performing with Technology

If you choose this option you will have the opportunity to use modern technology to compose, arrange and produce a piece of music. The two areas available to you are *MIDI Sequencing* and *Sound Engineering and Production*, each of which involve the recording and mixing (engineering) of music. This part of the course requires you to create a piece of music, or a folio of pieces, supported by a **session log** detailing procedures carried out, for example, each time you work in the recording studio or use the MIDI sequencer.

You will also prepare a short programme note for each composition/arrangement or recording you submit for assessment, and there will be a written/aural Knowledge and Understanding test lasting between 45 minutes and 1 hour. This test is based on either MIDI Sequencing or Sound Engineering and Production, depending on which of these options you have chosen, and will contain questions on terms used in these technologies. It will also include a number of recordings which you will listen to and then answer questions on (for instance, about the recording processes involved, or errors present).

You will normally undertake an assignment set by your teacher in which you are given a brief detailing the tasks to be completed in **either** MIDI Sequencing **or** Sound Engineering and Production. You might carry out these tasks by making an *arrangement* of another composer's work (from a score) or *composing* and/or *arranging* your own music.

During this assignment the teacher will assess and record your progress using an observation checklist.

Sound Engineering and Production

If you choose to undertake a project involving Sound Engineering and Production (the process of recording something and then altering or 'mixing' the resulting music), you will need to be familiar with a number of related terms, not only to help you operate equipment such as a mixing desk more efficiently, but also to prepare you for the Knowledge and Understanding test which forms part of the assessment for this area of the course (see **The Higher Music Qualification**, page 2).

The full range of terms, which includes those from previous grades, is listed below. (Don't be alarmed by the number of terms; many are fairly basic and easily understood.)

Sound Engineering and Production Terms at Higher Grade

Equipment, Technical Specifications, Processes, Techniques, Controls and Effects

AB Comparison – a technique which allows a studio engineer to switch between two or more devices or settings in order to compare them and identify any differences. For example, two microphones might be placed in different positions to record a singer, and using AB comparison the engineer can determine which microphone position is best.

Attack – this refers to the amount of time taken for a sound (or musical note) to reach its maximum initial volume or amplitude. For example, a bowed instrument will have a slower attack time than a percussive instrument such as a drum. The attack is the first part of the *envelope* of a sound (see **ADSR**, *Support Concepts*, page 33).

Balanced wiring connectors – audio cables which use balanced wiring (a wiring system which prevents interference from external sources such as radio waves).

Bouncing – a technique used in multi-track recording where two or more previously recorded tracks are 'bounced' onto a single track in order to free up space for more tracks to be recorded. This is normally done on 4- and 8-track recorders where space is limited.

Clipping – a form of distortion which occurs when a signal is too high for the electronic device it is connected to. It can damage equipment such as speakers. Clipping can be observed when input lights and meters flash red.

dB – an abbreviation of 'decibel', which is a unit of measurement of volume.

Decay – the second part of a sound envelope after the *attack*, the decay refers to the time when a sound is beginning to level off (*decay*) after maximum volume has been reached (*attack*) towards a more even volume (*sustain*).

Echo/reflection – an electronic effect which adds echo to an instrument/voice, making it sound as though it is being played in a room with this type of acoustic. The amount (or depth) of decay can be adjusted.

Enhancer/exciter – a dynamic processor which 'enhances' a signal to improve its sound quality by producing new frequencies which may have been lost during recording.

PERFORMING

Figure-of-eight mic – or 'bi-directional mic', this refers to a microphone that picks up signals well at both its front and rear, with a loss of sensitivity at the sides.

File compression – a means of compressing (making smaller) musical (or other) data, such as a MIDI file.

Graphic equaliser – a device which alters a sound using a number of preset filters, each of which can either *boost* or *attenuate* a band of frequencies around a *centre frequency* (each frequency band is normally adjusted using a slider control). Simpler equalisers have fewer bands (adjustable frequencies) and make basic adjustments to the amount of *bass* or *treble* in a sound, but 31-band equalisers are common for professional use, allowing far more subtle alterations to be made to sounds as well as reducing the possibility of *feedback*.

Insert point – often used for patching in dynamic processors to a mixing desk, this is a connection on a mixing desk (normally a single TRS jack) which transfers a signal from an input into an external processor (in order to alter it in some way) before it is returned again to a channel on the mixing desk.

Limiter – a dynamic processor which prevents a signal from exceeding a certain limit (or 'clipping') which could damage equipment such as speakers.

Parametric equaliser – an equaliser capable of *boosting* or *attenuating* any frequency range. It has three controls per filter: **gain** (to boost or attenuate the chosen frequencies); **sweep** (to choose the *centre* frequency of specific frequencies); and **bandwidth** or **Q control** (to increase or decrease the number of frequencies that are to be altered).

Phase cancellation – when two versions of the same signal cancel each other out (resulting in nothing) as the result of the peak of one waveform (signal) coinciding with the trough of another.

Phasing – an electronic effect which alters an original signal by delaying it and then playing it back on top of itself.

Pitch shift – a basic form of a harmoniser, this is a process which alters the pitch of a sound (signal) without altering its duration.

Post-fade – a signal which is either routed or monitored after it has passed through a channel fader and is consequently governed by the level of that channel fader.

Pre-fade – a signal which is independent of a channel fader position as it is either routed or monitored before it passes through the channel fader.

Ratio – a control on a *compressor* which manages the amount of compression applied to a signal after it exceeds the *threshold*.

Release – see ADSR, page 33.

Shelving equalisation – an equaliser filter which either boosts or attenuates continuously above or below a particular frequency.

Stereo pair – a pair of matched microphones (designated left and right) used for stereo recording where the signal from each mic is fed to two speakers (left and right).

Threshold – a control found on many dynamic processors which is used to establish the point where a specific process is used on a signal.

Unbalanced wiring connectors – audio cables which carry a signal through a single inner core, such as those used for jack-to-jack leads (for connecting an electric guitar to an amplifier, for example). These are more vulnerable to interference than *balanced wiring/connectors*.

Musical Features

Coda – an 'ending'; a section which concludes a piece of music.

Outro – a section which concludes (or 'plays out') a piece of music. The opposite of an intro, an outro can be regarded as another name for a Coda.

Sustain – the third part of a sound envelope (AD**S**R), this describes how long a note is held. For example, a note played by a wind instrument can be sustained for as long as the player exhales, whereas a note can be sustained constantly on a bowed instrument. A sustain effect processor can be added to an instrument such as an electric guitar to allow notes to be held for much longer than possible in normal playing.

Tempo/timing – the speed of a piece of music, often measured in beats per minute (BPM).

Tremolo – the very rapid repetition of a note, creating a warbling or trembling effect. Although the effect can be produced naturally by the player on most instruments, a tremolo effect processor can also be added to electronic instruments such as electric guitar and keyboards; this rapidly varies the volume up and down to reproduce the same effect.

Support Concepts

ADSR – abbreviation of *Attack*, *Decay*, *Sustain*, *Release*, which are the four parts of a sound envelope.

Active – a circuit which needs power in order to operate – for example, an effects pedal requiring battery power. *Passive* circuits do not require this type of power.

Balanced wiring – see *balanced wiring connectors*, page 31.

Bandpass filter (BPF) – a filter which functions as a kind of equaliser in that it stops the upper and lower frequencies of a signal and only lets through the middle 'band' of frequencies.

Centre frequency – the exact middle point of a frequency band, in between the top extreme of treble and the lower extreme of bass.

Crosstalk – when the signal from one track or channel is unintentionally transferred to another as the result of the two being too close together or one signal being at a very high level. Normally associated with analogue recording, the possibility of crosstalk is almost completely eliminated in digital recording.

DAT – abbreviation of *Digital Audio Tape*, which is a recordable digital tape similar in appearance to a video cassette. DAT has been generally superseded by CDs and MiniDiscs.

DSP – abbreviation of *Digital Signal Processing*, a technique which digitises a signal and alters it by adding other processes or digital signals to it.

High pass filter (HPF) – a filter which allows high frequencies to 'pass' through untouched whilst *attenuating* a range of lower frequencies.

Low pass filter (LPF) – a filter which allows lower frequencies to 'pass' through untouched whilst *attenuating* a range of higher frequencies.

Master – the final mixed version of a track or entire album which can be used to make mass produced copies.

Passive – a circuit which does not need power to operate – for example, the tone controls on an electric guitar.

Post-production – every aspect of what is done to a track/album after it has been recorded, including the *mixdown*, *mastering* and *mass production*.

Pre-production – everything involved in producing a piece of music before it is recorded, including composing, arranging, rehearsing and making studio arrangements.

Presence peak/colouration – the 'presence' of a strong mid-frequency (usually undesired) which 'colours' the sound; this can be caused by the frequency response or setup of a microphone (such as how close it is to a voice/instrument), faulty equipment, or even the acoustic effect of the room.

Q/bandwidth – the range (width) of frequencies affected by an *equalisation* filter. Q simply means 'quality factor' and refers to whether the bandwidth filter is *narrow* and of High quality (affecting a small range of frequencies), or *wide* and of Low quality (affecting a larger range of frequencies).

Red book standard – a standard for audio CDs defined by Sony and Philips in the 1980s which indicates the basic format for CD audio reproduction (including the dimensions of the disc, the *sample rate* and *bit depth*, and the maximum playing time). The need for this specific distinction arose when CDs came to be used not only for audio but also as a means of storing data; consequently there are various 'book colours' which describe other formats.

Slave – a piece of equipment which reacts to (and is therefore controlled by) information sent by a master device.

SPL – an abbreviation of *Sound Pressure Level*, this refers to the acoustic pressure of a sound wave which is measured in decibels (dB). A loud sound, for example, has a high SPL.

Squawker – a speaker in a *loudspeaker* cabinet which only deals with mid frequencies.

Submix – an individual sound which has been mixed, but is in itself part of a larger mix. For example, a synthesizer track in a song may have been mixed to produce a specific sound, but that sound will be only one of many which will be mixed during the mastering process.

Sweep – a control found on *parametric* and *semi-parametric equalisers* which establishes the *centre frequency* of the filter.

Synchronisation (Sync.) – when musical tracks or devices playing together at the same time play in perfect time with each other.

Transducer – an electronic device which converts one kind of energy into another (these include microphones and amplifiers).

Transient – a loud and brief signal which has a very rapid *attack* and *decay* time.

TRS jack – a jack plug and socket in which there are three parts to the connection (as with an electric guitar): *Tip*, *Ring* and *Sleeve* (TRS). The Tip can *send* a signal from an insert point on one device to another (e.g. guitar to amplifier), the Ring being the *return*, while the Sleeve, which is common to both signals, is connected to *ground* or *earth*.

Waveform – a signal or sound wave represented as a graph.

Wavelength – the length between the matching points of successive sound waves. High-frequency sound waves have short wavelengths, and low-frequency waves have long wavelengths.

Sound Engineering and Production Terms used in Previous Grades Equipment, Technical Specifications, Processes, Techniques, Controls and Effects		
From Access 3 level	**From Intermediate 1 level**	**From Intermediate 2 level**
Amplifier	Balance	AFL/Solo
CD	Buss	Analogue
Channel	Cardioid or uni-directional	Auxiliary send/return
Connector	microphone	Boost (EQ)
Count-in	Click track	Chorus (effect)
Distortion	Close mic'd	Compressor
Dry	DI (box)	Condenser microphone
Echo	Effects unit/processor	Delay (effect)
Fader	Equalisation (EQ)	Digital
Fade-in	Final mix	Dynamic mic
Fade-out	Foldback	Dynamic range
Gain	Mixing desk/Mixer	EQ cut
Headphones (cans)	Monitor	Feedback
Input	Multi-track	Filter
Jack plug	Mute/cut	Frequency response
Lead/cable	Omni-directional microphone	Impedance
Level	Overdrive	Leakage
Loudspeaker	Overdub	Line level
Meter	Pan(ning)	Mic level
Microphone	Peak	Noise gate
Microphone stand	Popping/blasting	PFL
Mix (down)	Pop-shield	Phantom power
Mono(phonic)	Reverb(eration)	Proximity effect/bass tip up
Noise	Stereo master	Punch in/out (Drop in/out)
Output	Talkback	Sibilance
Phono plug/connector	Time domain effects	Signal chain/path
Recorder	Windshield	Spillage
Session log	XLR	
Stereo(phonic)		
Track		
Trim		
Wet		

Support Concepts		
From Access 3 level	**From Intermediate 1 level**	**From Intermediate 2 level**
Acoustic	Ambience	Attenuate
Acoustic screen	Boom (stand)	Autolocate
Arrangement	Cue	Effects loop (FX)
Circuit breaker	Direct sound	Foldback
Control room	Earth/ground	Gated reverb
Live room	Indirect sound	Hard-disk recorder
Mains multi-block	Master fader	I/O
Record	MIDI	Masking
Session	Overdrive	MiniDisc (MD)
Signal	Overload	Patchbay
Take	Pick-up	Patchlead
Tape	Pick-up pattern	Signal-to-noise ratio
Tone control	Remix	(S/N ratio)
Track sheets	Stage monitor	Shock mount
Two-track recorder	Tracking	Sub-group
(2-track)		Sub-woofer
		Synchronisation (Sync)
		Tweeter
		Woofer

Other musical features		
Backing vocals	Acoustic guitar	Bridge
Bass guitar	Chorus (in a song structure)	Key change/modulation
Drum kit	Dynamics/Expression	Middle 8
Guitar	Electric guitar	Pitch bend
Introduction	Flat	Rhythms
Lead vocal	Guide vocal	Texture
Riff	Solo	
Synthesizer	Verse	
Vocals	Wah-wah	

MIDI Sequencing

Note: for practice and further information on MIDI sequencing, see **Arranging and Composing**, page 41.

If you have chosen to undertake a MIDI project as one of your Higher Music Performing options, you will need to be familiar with a range of MIDI sequencing terms from both Higher Music and earlier grades, all of which are listed below.

MIDI Sequencing Terms at Higher Grade

Aftertouch – a way of producing a control signal on a MIDI keyboard, determined by the amount of pressure applied to the keys. Aftertouch can control functions such as loudness, sustain and filter brightness.

Analogue – a piece of electronic equipment whose acoustic signal is produced by a changing current or voltage.

dB – an abbreviation of 'decibel', which is a unit of measurement for the amount of volume produced by a device.

Delay – the amount of time between an original electronic signal and its repetition, creating an echo effect. The duration and repetition of the delay (echo) can be almost infinitely varied using a digital delay processor.

Distortion – when an amplified sound becomes distorted as a result of a setting which is too high (especially volume). Although essentially an unwanted sound, it is often used intentionally as an effect, especially on electric guitar in hard rock and heavy metal music.

Dry – an electronic signal (sound) that has had no effect added to it.

Expression – using Continuous Controller 11, this facility is used to produce aspects of musical expression such as crescendos, diminuendos and general dynamic range.

Glitch – a slight technical problem which suddenly occurs with a piece of equipment – for example, a distorted sound or a temporary disruption of a signal.

Hiss – a continuous high frequency noise produced by electronic audio devices. At high volume levels, speakers often produce an audible hiss.

Noise – non-musical sounds produced by electronic equipment, such as hissing, humming or feedback, often as a result of interference or levels which are set too high.

Nudge – a MIDI function which allows notes and audio files to be moved forwards or backwards in time by set amounts.

Pitch shifter – a device (often found on synthesizers and MIDI keyboards) which changes the pitch of an audio signal (note) without affecting its duration.

Polyphony – when more than one note is played at the same time by a device or a musical instrument; these are called 'polyphonic' instruments, as opposed to 'monophonic' instruments which are only capable of playing a single note at a time.

Portamento – when pitch is changed in a smooth, gliding manner from one pitch to another as the keys are pressed (or MIDI notes sent).

Sample – a sound which has been recorded (sometimes from an existing music CD) and digitised (sampled) in order that it can be used, for example, in a sampler or played at various pitches on a synthesizer.

Synchronisation – the process of synchronising sounds: matching them in time with each other, or with film.

Transient – a quick, loud signal which has a rapid *attack* and *decay* time.

Wet – an electronic signal (sound) that has been altered or enhanced by the use of an effect.

Support Concepts

Automated mixing – a process where a mix is stored and used later in either *real-time* or *snapshot* mode on a computer, which means that an engineer can adjust parameters during a mix and save them on the computer, which can then play those adjustments in complete synchronisation with the actual music playback.

Bank – a selection of sounds – found in a synthesizer or sound card – within a particular category: for example, classical guitar, electric guitar, jazz guitar, etc.

Frequency response – the measure of frequency range that an electrical device can deal with.

Groove – a specific stylistic rhythm pattern (for example, swing, tango, etc.) which can be applied to a basic rhythm in a MIDI sequence and so alter it without the need to re-enter any notes.

Latency – the time (delay) taken for a signal to enter a processor and come out again. Latency is more evident in recordings where computers are involved, as it is affected by the speed of the computer's processor.

Overload – to go beyond the safe or normal operating capacity of an electrical or electronic circuit.

Peak – the highest signal level registered on a mixer/mixing desk by a particular voice/instrument.

Playlist – the order in which music files (tracks) are to be played on a computer's media player or a device such as an MP3 player.

Plug-in – software which does not operate on its own but as part of another computer program – for example, a software synthesizer.

Sample editor – a program used to edit small audio samples taken from existing recordings such as music CDs.

Sample frequency – The digital frequency of a sound sample.

Scrub – a tool found on a sequencer which is used to move to various points in a track by playing back or moving backwards or forwards at any chosen speed.

Softsynth – another name for a 'software synthesizer', which is a MIDI software program that contains extra sound-sets/effects for use with a MIDI sequencer.

Truncate – to shorten a track or a sound by removing part of it.

VST – abbreviation of *Virtual Studio Technology*, which is a plug-in standard (developed by Steinberg).

VST instrument – an audio instrument or software synthesizer which conforms to the VST standard (see *VST*).

Equipment

MiniDisc (MD) – resembling a small CD, the MiniDisc is a medium which uses compression software in order to store lots of digital, optical, record-and-read information.

Mixer – a device used for 'mixing' the sound (timbre, volume, etc.) of individual tracks, as well as balancing the combined sound of several tracks played in combination.

MP3 – abbreviation of *Moving Pictures Executive Group Level-1 Layer 3*, which is a digital data compression format which greatly reduces the size of an audio file, allowing it to be downloaded quickly via the Internet or stored on an MP3 player – which can, for example, hold several hundred songs.

Support Concept

Firewire – an interface which permits the exchange of data between a computer and other devices such as video cameras.

MIDI Sequencing Terms used in Previous Grades		
From Access 3 level	**From Intermediate 1 level**	**From Intermediate 2 level**
Arrange window	Backup copy	Chorus depth
BPM (beats per minute)	Balance	Chorus (effect)
Copy/Cut and paste	Boot	Coda
Count-in	Chorus (in a song structure)	Digital
Event	Controller keyboard	Fade in
Local control	Dynamics/expression	Fade out
Metronome/click	Effects (FX)	Fader
MIDI	General MIDI	Introduction
MIDI files	Import/Export	Local
MIDI In	Introduction	Key command
MIDI Out	Key change/Modulation	Master fader
Mix/Balance	Level	Merge
Panning	Locators	Middle 8
Record	Loop	Mix (or mixdown)
Save	Markers	Mono(phonic)
Silence	MIDI channel	Multi-timbral
Tempo	MIDI Thru	Note off
Time signature	Modulation controller	Note on
Track (names)	Mute	Outro
Transport bar/controls	Octave	Overdub
Undo	Pitch	Pitch bend
Velocity	Programme change	Punch In/Out (Drop In/Out)
Volume	Quantisation	Real time
	Reset controller	Remix
	Reverb(eration)	Rhythms
	Snap	Stereo(phonic)
	Solo	Tremolo
	Sustain	
	Time signature	
	Track list	
	Transpose	
	Verse	

Support Concepts		
From Access 3 level	**From Intermediate 1 level**	**From Intermediate 2 level**
Application	Cycle/loop modes	Continuous controller
File management	Input	Cycle/loops mode
Format	Note number	GS (General Standard MIDI)
Signal	Output	MIDI implementation chart
Toolbox	Parameter	Step-time recording
	Patch	
	Production log	
	Timbre	
	Track object	
	Zoom in/out	

Equipment Terms		
Amplifier	CD-R	XG (soundcards)
Headphones	CD-RW	
Interface	GM mixer	
Loudspeaker	Phono connector	
MIDI interface	USB	
Sequencer		
Synthesizer		

ARRANGING AND COMPOSING

This chapter contains arranging and composing workshops based on four contrasting pieces of music.

- ◆ The first workshop is an exercise involving a traditional folk melody, in which you will be introduced to a number of arranging and MIDI sequencing techniques.
- ◆ The second workshop focuses on an instrumental piece in **rondo** form which is built upon a **ground bass**.
- ◆ The third is a **modal Scots Song** with piano accompaniment.
- ◆ The fourth is a jazz piece in an **improvised** style with an **ostinato** accompaniment.

Each workshop gives you the opportunity to put into practice a wide range of composing techniques as well as the concepts you will have encountered both in the Higher Music course and earlier grades.

Working through these workshops has several advantages:

- ◆ You will acquire a better understanding and more thorough knowledge of the musical concepts featured.
- ◆ You will have the opportunity to see these concepts 'at work' in a piece of music.
- ◆ Working and composing with a range of musical concepts will help you to identify them more quickly by ear, which is an essential skill for your Listening assessments and final written exam.
- ◆ You will learn a number of composing methods and techniques for creating interesting, well-structured and professional-sounding music.
- ◆ The workshops combine several of the main elements which are part of the Higher Music course, namely *musical concepts, composing, arranging, MIDI sequencing, mixing* and, if you take part in a live performance of any of your compositions, *performing* too.

The order in which you work through these workshops isn't important, but there is a slightly ascending level of complexity, with workshop 4 being the most challenging. However, you should find that the step-by-step approach to composing/arranging in the workshops makes all of them fairly straightforward.

Note: MIDI sequencing features in workshops 1, 3 and 4. Workshops 1 and 4 can be used specifically as MIDI sequencing projects.

Workshop 1: Arranging 'Scarborough Fair'

Although essentially a MIDI sequencing workshop, many of the instrumental **arranging** techniques described in the following exercise can also be used for live instruments, and therefore apply to any project which involves the arrangement of a piece of music. Those who have chosen the *Sound Engineering and Production* option might also find the workshop helpful.

In this section, you will arrange a traditional folk melody using a MIDI sequencer. Depending on your level of experience with this type of music software, the exercise will either introduce you to some effective techniques for composing and arranging with the sequencer, or give you a little extra practice with them.

If you have chosen the *Performing with Technology* option, completion of this workshop will also provide you with a piece of music which can be added to your folio.

Before we begin the workshop, let's review some of the ways in which the MIDI sequencer can be used for arranging and composing.

Advantages of using a MIDI sequencer

Working with a MIDI sequencer means that composers and arrangers can perform the following tasks:

◆ Produce a piece of music which is complete in itself.

◆ **Arrange** a piece of music for different instruments or sound patches.

◆ Use a MIDI keyboard or computer mouse to input a complete piece of music (even a full orchestral score), and then use the MIDI sequencer to **arrange** the music, play it back and finally record it onto CD.

◆ Print out the music notation of a composition/arrangement for the use of musicians in a live performance.

◆ Some sequencing packages can scan music from a printed score into the sequencer, where it can then be edited, arranged and recorded like any other piece of music.

◆ **Remix** a piece of music.

◆ Hear what a section of music or an entire piece might sound like when performed by live instruments.

◆ Compose a piece of music.

◆ Hear what different parts and **harmonies** sound like when played together, such as a **melody** with **chords**, or a **melody** and a **counter-melody**.

◆ Print out a full score and/or individual parts.

Capabilities of the MIDI sequencer

The sequencer has 127 preset sounds or 'patches' (collectively known as the 'MIDI sound set') which provide a wide range of sampled sounds ranging from 'natural' instruments (such as *grand piano, flute, cello, bass guitar*) and electronic sounds (*synth strings, pad 2 warm, calliope lead, new age*) to drum and percussion sounds (*timpani, drum kit, tubular bells, xylophone*) and even sound effects (*bird tweet, sea shore, applause, helicopter*).

There are 16 channels (or tracks) on which you can record *different* sounds, using either patches from the MIDI sound set or live instruments, but you have another 111 'spare' channels on which any one of the sounds you have used in the first 16 channels can be used again. For example, if you have assigned an *acoustic grand piano* patch to play a melody on track 1, you can use the same patch on tracks 17, 18, 19 and 20 (more if you want) and still have another 15 tracks (from the first 16) on which to record new sounds.

This technology means you can build up the texture of a piece of music fairly quickly by having several instrument sounds (patches) play the **melody, chords, arpeggios** and **bass** part simultaneously, in addition to adding drums and even sound effects. You can also record (or **overdub**) 'live' sound sources (such as vocals or musical instruments) to play alongside the electronically produced music.

It is also possible to record something on, say, tracks 2–7 using five different sound patches and then **mix** this music and finally record it again onto a *single* spare track (track 21, for instance). This technique, known as *bouncing*, allows you to free up some of those important first 16 channels again (channels 2–7 in this case) on which new sounds can then be recorded.

The possibilities for creating a piece of music with many layers of different sounds and overdubs are therefore almost limitless.

Many sequencing packages have sample sound files (pieces of music created using the sequencer) which demonstrate various instrumental combinations (such as *wind quintet*, *orchestra*, *rock group*, *pop group* and so on), allowing you to hear what can be achieved with the software. If you can, listen to a selection of these files to give yourself some ideas before starting any new piece of music with the sequencer.

Assigning different MIDI sound patches to each track

When you record/compose a piece of music on a sequencer, each track will usually correspond to a separate part of your composition or arrangement. For instance, if you are arranging a song which consists of a melody accompanied by keyboard, guitar, bass guitar and drums, these five parts will each have to be given a separate track on the sequencer. Such an arrangement is straightforward: you could use tracks 1, 2, 3 and 4 for the melody, keyboard, guitar and bass guitar parts, and channel 10 (normally reserved for MIDI drum and percussion sounds) for the drum track.

Choosing MIDI sound patches

As a rough guide, when choosing instruments/sound patches, you should split your piece into three sections: top, middle and bottom. The top part represents the most prominent or highest pitched notes (the main melody, for example), the bottom is the bass, and the middle part is the 'fill in', where harmonic instruments (those capable of playing chords) can expand the texture. Next, make a list of the instrument sounds you might like to have in your piece and put these into the category (top, middle or bottom) which best suits their pitch. You can sketch a diagram like the one below to represent this.

TOP (melody)
Piccolo, Flute, Clarinet, Oboe, Violin, Electric guitar, Glockenspiel
MIDDLE ('fill in' – chords, arpeggios)
Piano, Keyboard, Harp, Acoustic guitar, Organ, Strings
BOTTOM (bass and drums)
Bass guitar, Cello, Double bass, Drum kit/percussion

Once you have recorded a track into the sequencer, you can hear what it will sound like when played on different instruments by selecting the *loop* function (this will play the track in a constantly repeating cycle until you press *stop* or deselect the *loop*), then, as the track is playing back in a loop, select different sound patches by scrolling down the various patches in the track properties menu. Doing this means you can try out any number of sounds without having the interruption of resetting the track back to the start each time it comes to an end.

Combining MIDI sound patches

To hear what a track sounds like when played by two or more MIDI sound patches simultaneously, simply select the track (which, let's say, you have assigned to channel 1), then *copy* and *paste* it into any number of the other free channels. You now have two or more channels (or tracks) which will play the same music in perfect **unison**, to which you can assign different patches from the MIDI sound set.

This process will build up the depth of a **melody** (or any other part) and alter its **timbre**, and again you can use the *loop* function on playback to experiment with numerous different sound combinations in the manner described above.

MIDI percussion and sound effects

In addition to **pitched percussion** instruments such as *xylophone*, *glockenspiel*, *vibraphone* and so on, which can be used for either **melody** or **harmony**, there are a number of **unpitched percussion** sounds available on MIDI sequencers which can add a professional touch to your piece. A *cymbal* played **on the beat** will add extra drama to a **crescendo**; a *woodblock* can sound like a ticking clock (or bones rattling!); and there are plenty of other sound effects such as *applause*, *seashore*, *bird tweet*, *telephone* and even *helicopter* which you might be able to incorporate into your piece to create something a bit unusual. Also don't forget that the sequencer will allow you to alter the **pitch** and **timbre** of all these sounds – at the touch of a button – in ways that aren't always possible with real instruments, giving you even more potential to produce something really original.

Hints and Tips

Pitched percussion instrument sounds like *xylophone*, *glockenspiel*, *vibraphone*, *marimba* and *tubular bells* can be used to great effect in both the **melody** and **accompaniment** parts of an arrangement.

The importance of volume levels

An important aspect of arranging a piece of music for many instruments or sound patches on the sequencer is the individual volume of each of these. Some instrument sounds are naturally louder or have a timbre which gives them greater prominence than others, which means they will overpower other quieter, more subtle sounds unless the volume levels are **mixed down** to balance everything out. Not only will the various *sounds* of different instruments in combination produce a new single sound, but so will their individual *volume* levels. Setting and re-setting the volume levels until you are absolutely happy with the result is an aspect of arranging/mixing which requires some time and patience, but you will be rewarded with some great sounds.

Arranging a traditional folk song: 'Scarborough Fair'

The music for *Scarborough Fair*, a traditional folk melody, is shown on page 45. As is common with the way a lot of folk music appears in books, only the melody and guitar chords are given. But don't worry, the important information you need to make a really good arrangement of the piece is all there on the page!

I have arranged this piece myself using a MIDI sequencer, but rather than take you through the arrangement one step at a time as I do in the composing workshops, here I am going to show you a number of helpful arranging techniques and let you experiment with these as you develop your own arrangement. It will probably be more beneficial to you if you don't listen to my finished arrangement on CD track 38 until *after* you have completed your own, as there is the risk that you will be tempted to copy much of what you hear rather than work out your own ideas. However, if you decide to change something in the first version of your completed arrangement after listening to mine, that's fine.

Arranging techniques

Here are some arranging techniques you might use to develop the basic melody of 'Scarborough Fair' into a full arrangement for a number of instruments or MIDI sound patches.

The Melody – the 'Top' part of the arrangement

Using several different instruments or MIDI sound patches to play the **melody** of your piece in **unison** not only gives you the opportunity to create your own unique sound, but will also add depth and texture to the melody. And don't forget, when combining sounds in this way a whole new **timbre** can be created simply by adjusting the volume levels of each instrument/patch.

Here are some techniques that you might use for arranging the melody:

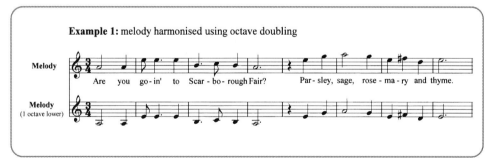

Example 1: melody harmonised using octave doubling

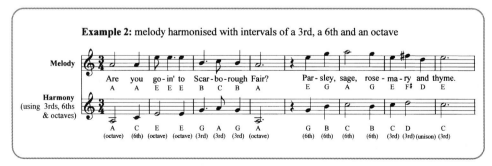

Example 2: melody harmonised with intervals of a 3rd, a 6th and an octave

The Chord Accompaniment – the 'Middle' part of the arrangement

Here are some techniques that you might use for arranging the chords/accompaniment:

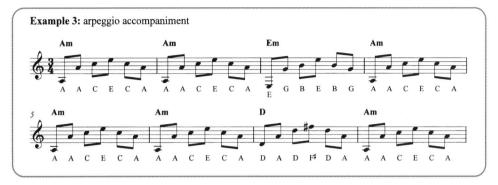

Example 3: arpeggio accompaniment

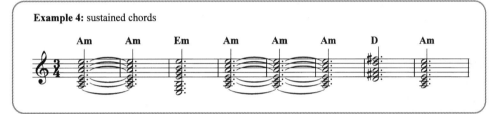

Example 4: sustained chords

The Bass – the 'Bottom' part of the arrangement

Here are some techniques that you might use for arranging/composing a bass part:

Example 5: bass guitar (simple)

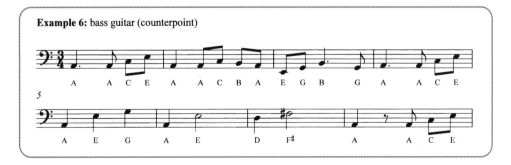

Example 6: bass guitar (counterpoint)

MIDI Drums and Percussion

Using *drum kit* and other percussion sounds will bring most pieces to life, especially songs, by providing a steady beat which helps to drive the music and give it extra depth. However, some music, such as 'Scarborough Fair', may sound better without the addition of a drum part, and therefore I haven't included one in my arrangement of the piece, but of course you may do so if you like. For some guidelines on working with MIDI drum and percussion sounds refer to Workshop 4, page 105.

Building the texture in specific areas

There are parts of a piece of music, such as the **chorus** in a song, where you will probably want to make the sound 'bigger'. There are a few ways to do this.

◆ Increase the volume of some or all of the tracks.

◆ Change some of the instruments/sound patches on the tracks.

◆ Add some extra tracks with new instruments/sound patches.

Here are the first eight bars of my own arrangement of 'Scarborough Fair' showing the texture of the music and the sound patches used for each track. The *String Ensemble* part is silent until the second verse begins – the entry of this new sound (which plays sustained chords) makes the sound 'bigger' in verse 2. You will hear this happening when you come to listen to the arrangement on CD track 38 (*00.28*).

Here is a chart showing the tracks used in my arrangement of 'Scarborough Fair', together with the sound patches used, individual volume levels and musical material played. All of these sounds can be found on any MIDI sequencer.

TRACK	PATCH (sound)	VOLUME (max = 127)	MUSIC PLAYED
1	**Pan flute**	100	**Main melody**
2	**French horn**	70	**Harmony** in 3rds, 6ths and octaves
3	**Synth. voice**	40	**Main melody** (played an octave lower)
4	**Harpsichord**	35	**Arpeggio** accompaniment
5	**Synth. strings 2**	40	**Chords**
6	**String ensemble**	35	**Chords**
7	**Electric bass guitar (finger)**	50	**Bass counterpoint**

Arranging for live instruments

If you were arranging 'Scarborough Fair' for performance on live instruments instead of a MIDI sequencer, many of the arranging processes would be the same but with one very important extra consideration: you would have to ensure that the **pitch** of the notes given to a particular instrument were within the playing **range** of that instrument. Whilst this is not an issue when using a sequencer (indeed, some interesting effects can be created on a sequencer when a sound patch plays notes that are higher or lower than would be possible on the *real* instrument), it is something which becomes of the utmost significance if you intend to score your piece for a live performance – and equally live musicians! You can check the ranges of individual instruments in a music dictionary or a music theory book such as *The AB Guide to Music Theory, Part 2,* published by the Associated Board (contact details on page 6).

Transposing instruments

Another important consideration when composing or arranging a piece of music for live instruments is whether or not you will be using any **transposing instruments**. These are instruments whose written notes are different from their sounding notes, and therefore the notes you want such instruments to play have to be **transposed** up or down a certain **interval** (depending on the instrument) to accommodate this factor.

There are several different kinds of transposing instruments, including the clarinet, trumpet, horn and double bass, whose sounding pitches are all different from so-called 'concert pitch.'

For example, the most commonly used clarinet is the B♭ clarinet, which is pitched **one tone** lower than standard concert pitch (taking the note C as your guide, B♭ is **one tone** lower than C).

This might seem confusing, but all you have to do to get the B♭ clarinet to play the notes you have written is **transpose** them up a **tone** (you can do this either on manuscript paper or using a sequencer, the latter of which will perform the task for you with a few clicks of the computer's mouse).

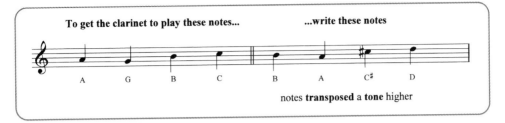

You will notice in the above example that there is a C♯ in the transposed version. In some musical scores, **accidentals** are written on the transposing instrument's part where required in the music, but it is more common also to **transpose** the **key signature** as well. So, if a piece of music is in the key of C major, the **key signature** for the B♭ clarinet part would go up a **tone** to D major (which has a key signature of F♯ and C♯), thus preventing the need to write sharp signs every time an F♯ or C♯ occurs.

You therefore need to find out what **key** the instrument is in (in relation to the note C) and **transpose** your music accordingly. Here are a few examples of common transposing instruments:

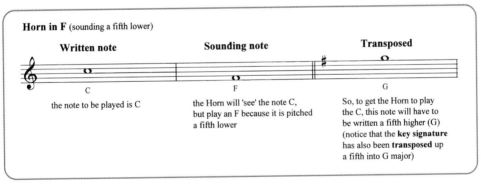

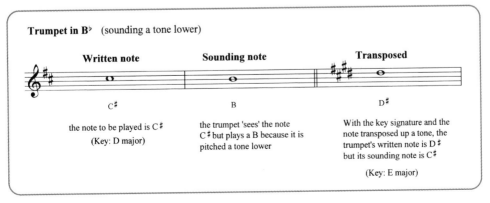

ARRANGING AND COMPOSING

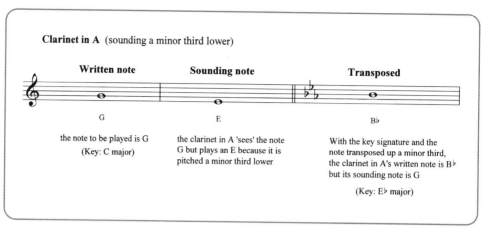

Clarinet in A (sounding a minor third lower)

Written note	Sounding note	Transposed
G	E	B♭
the note to be played is G (Key: C major)	the clarinet in A 'sees' the note G but plays an E because it is pitched a minor third lower	With the key signature and the note transposed up a minor third, the clarinet in A's written note is B♭ but its sounding note is G (Key: E♭ major)

This process is the same for nearly all transposing instruments – one exception being instruments such as the double bass, whose notes sound an **octave** lower than written but are not transposed on the musical stave.

Workshop 2: Composing 'Dance Rondo'

In this composing workshop, together we will create a piece of instrumental music in **rondo** form which uses musical concepts encountered in Higher Music as well as some from earlier grades. As you probably know, before starting work on any new composition it helps to have as many ideas as possible about the kind of piece you would like to write, including the musical elements (or concepts) that you might include. You should consider things like:

◆ **What, if anything, is the piece about?**

◆ **What will be its style/structure?**

◆ **Which instrument(s) is the piece being written for?**

◆ **What will be the tonality – major, minor, atonal?**

◆ **Will it modulate into another key or several different keys?**

◆ **What musical concepts might be used?**

◆ **Approximately how long will it last?**

It is also a good idea to listen to and analyse several pieces of music which are similar in style to the one you would like to write, and note how these compositions have been put together.

Of course, you don't need to have a *strict* plan for your piece before you begin – you might start off by **improvising** and just let the music 'grow' out of spontaneous musical ideas – but working to a plan has several advantages:

◆ It can make the composing process more straightforward for you.

◆ It ensures that your completed piece will be well structured.

◆ You will learn more about the musical form you are writing in (in this case, **rondo**), which will help you to identify that form more easily when you *hear* it – a useful skill for Listening tests!

◆ It could make it much easier for you to build up a larger-scale piece of music.

The two main structural elements I will be using in this workshop are **rondo** form and a **ground bass**. I would like you to do the same, composing your own rondo one section at a time as I take you through my composition processes step-by-step. (You may want to revise *rondo* form and *ground bass* before going any further.)

Writing a piece in rondo form will enable you to build a bigger composition by piecing several smaller sections together – and what's more, you will be sure from the very start that your completed piece will have a sound structure.

Step 1: The plan

Below are my rough notes for the rondo, beginning with six main 'framework' elements, followed by a list of musical concepts I might use in the piece, and then a basic structure plan.

Six main framework elements

1   **Rondo form** (ABACA)

2   **Ground bass**

3   **Three instrumental parts** (a *trio*): **melody** (for a *solo* instrument such as violin, flute or clarinet); **chord accompaniment** (for a *harmonic* instrument such as guitar, keyboard or piano); **ground bass** (for a *bass* instrument such as cello or bass guitar)

4   **3/4 time** (*triple metre*)

5   **Lively tempo** (*allegro*)

6   **Major key** (*D major*), **modulating** to other keys in the contrasting **episodes**

Concepts I might use

- Syncopation
- Suspensions
- Ornaments (grace note, mordent, trill, etc.)
- Appoggiaturas
- Stepwise and leaping melodies
- Passing notes
- Variation
- Melodic and harmonic sequence
- Tierce de Picardie
- Hemiola
- Key modulations

- Chromaticism
- Dominant 7th chords
- Cross rhythms
- Contrary motion
- Counterpoint
- Coda
- Chord inversions
- Pizzicato
- Staccato
- Pedal
- Varied dynamics

Structure plan

A SECTION	B SECTION	A SECTION	C SECTION	A SECTION
Tonic key (*D major*)	Relative minor key (*B minor*)	Tonic key (*D major*)	Dominant key (*A major*)	Tonic key (*D major*)
8–12 bars of music, consisting of 2 or 3 melodic phrases	8–12 bars (2–3 phrases) containing some ideas (fragments of **rhythm** or **melody**) used in the A section	**Repeat** of the A section but played an **octave** lower this time to create some **variation**	Perhaps longer than the other sections (12–16 bars), to further **develop** the musical ideas used previously	**Repeat** of the A section at its original **pitch**, with a small **Coda** (2–6 bars long)

For Practice

Using my notes and structure plan as a guide, make a plan for your own rondo now.

Step 2: Taking the plan a stage further

Having made notes for the structure and style of the piece, we can now take a closer look at the **chords** used in the key(s) we intend to use for the rondo, as these can help to determine our choice of **melody** notes as well as the **harmony**. Writing down all of these chords (and their individual notes) on a piece of music manuscript (or printing them out using music software) will mean we have an excellent reference source while composing the piece. Below is an example of the kind of diagram you might make for every key you want to use.

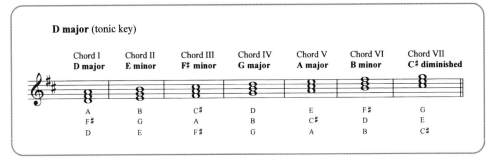

You can also experiment with **inversions** of the chords. For example:

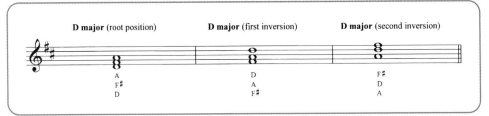

For Practice

On a piece of music manuscript paper, or using a computer, write/print out all the chords (including, of course, their individual notes) found in the keys you intend to use in your rondo, perhaps also writing their **inversions** too. Remember that you can add 7ths to your basic **triads** (3-note chords) – e.g. the **dominant 7th** chord.

With all of the above information at hand, we now have a lot of material to guide us as we write the rondo. So let's start composing!

Step 3: Composing the Ground Bass

Although it might be more common practice to write a **melody** and then **harmonise** it with **chords**, or write a chord progression and compose (or improvise) a melody on top of those chords, I am going to begin my rondo by composing the **ground bass** first, as this is the main structural element (the 'backbone') of the whole piece.

Ground Bass figure

D   F♯   A   D   A   F♯

As you can see, I have kept it short and simple. It is a 2-bar figure which uses the **chord notes** of D major (D, F♯, A). I may decide to alter the ground bass in places as I write the melody of my rondo, but this simple 2-bar figure will nevertheless form the basis of the entire composition.

CD track 39. You can hear this 2-bar ground bass figure played in a 'loop' (repeated several times) on CD track 39.

For Practice

Start off your rondo by composing a short **ground bass** that can be **repeated** over and over to form the foundation of the piece. Remember that, since the ground bass will be repeated constantly, it can consist of a couple of bars or just a few notes.

Step 4: Writing the first melodic phrase

Now I'm going to compose the first **melodic phrase** of the A section of my rondo. In my structure plan I estimated that the A section would be between 8 and 12 bars long, so I might have either two or three 4-bar phrases, depending on what I come up with as I compose.

To generate ideas for a **melody**, I **improvised** in the key of D major over the **ground bass**, and also experimented with **intervals** which are a *third*, a *sixth* and an *octave* apart from the notes in the ground bass.

Below is the first melodic phrase, 4 bars in length, of the A section of my rondo. Notice that the phrase is based on just two notes of the D major chord (D and F#) and a **passing note** (E). Can you see how **intervals** of a *third* and a *sixth* have been used between the ground bass and melody notes? You will also notice that, even though these intervals occur, the distance between bass and treble notes is more than two **octaves**. When intervals are more than an octave apart they are known as *compound* intervals (e.g. compound thirds, compound sixths). The **interval** between the D in the bass and the F# in the melody on the first beat of bar 1 is therefore a *compound third*.

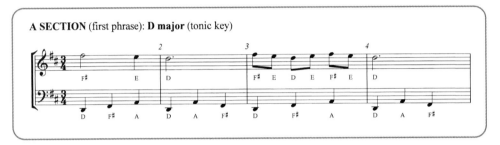

A SECTION (first phrase): **D major** (tonic key)

CD track 40. You can hear this 4-bar melodic phrase played over the ground bass on CD track 40.

My entire rondo will 'grow' from this simple opening phrase and ground bass figure since the musical material that follows will be influenced by both of these elements. You will see how this happens as the piece develops.

For Practice

Start composing the first **melodic phrase** of your own rondo now. You might choose to do this by **improvising** over your ground bass as it is played back to you (by a fellow student, or using a keyboard or MIDI sequencer), or by working out **melody** notes that will **harmonise** with it. If you use the latter method, remember that **intervals** of a *third*, a *sixth* and an *octave* will give you a nice harmony, but **appoggiaturas**, **chromatic notes**, **passing notes** and dissonant notes (**dissonance**) can also produce good effects. Experiment until you really like what you hear.

Step 5: Completing the A section

I now have to continue on from the first melodic phrase and complete the melody for the whole A section. To do this I will play the first phrase over repeatedly to see what other music might spring into mind (the best ideas often come this way!), and experiment with notes from other chords in the key of D major.

CD Track 41. Below is the music for my completed A section, which you can hear on CD track 41, followed by a brief written summary of how it was put together.

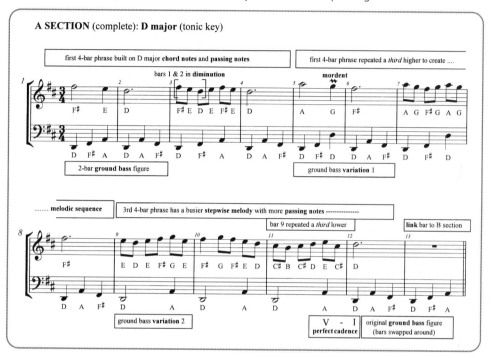

A SECTION (complete): **D major** (tonic key)

first 4-bar phrase built on D major **chord notes** and **passing notes**

first 4-bar phrase repeated a *third* higher to create ....

bars 1 & 2 in **diminution**

mordent

2-bar **ground bass** figure

ground bass **variation** 1

.... **melodic sequence**

3rd 4-bar phrase has a busier **stepwise melody** with more **passing notes** --------------

bar 9 repeated a *third* lower

link bar to B section

ground bass **variation** 2

V – I
perfect cadence

original **ground bass** figure
(bars swapped around)

A SECTION: D Major (tonic key)			
	Bars 1–4	**Bars 5–8**	**Bars 9–13**
Melody	First 4-bar phrase is based on three **descending stepwise** notes (F♯, E and D). D and F♯ are taken from the key chord, D major; the E is an *accented* **passing note** in bar 1; and an *unaccented* **passing note** in bar 3.	First 4-bar phrase is repeated a *third* higher (**melodic sequence**). A **mordent** (ornament) is added to the G in bar 5. **Stepwise** movement has now been established as a feature of the melody.	New 4-bar phrase in which shorter note values and **passing notes** create a busier melody that ends with a **perfect cadence** (V–I) in bar 12.
Bass	Simple 2-bar **ground bass** figure using the **chord notes** of D major (D, F♯, A).	**Ground bass** is **varied**, but still uses D major **chord notes**.	**Ground bass** is **varied** again in bars 9–11; this time the **rhythm** is changed and F♯ is not used. In bars 12 and 13 the original 2-bar ground bass returns, but the order of the bars is swapped around so that the last note in bar 13 is an A, which will make a smooth **link** onto the first bass note of the 'B' section (this will be a B).

Since the A section will be **repeated** twice more in the overall structure of the rondo, the piece is therefore more than half finished already!

For Practice

Complete the melody for the A section of your own rondo, using the opening phrase to help you compose the music which will follow. You might look at ways in which you can re-use elements from this first phrase (**rhythm**, **melody** fragments, note groupings, etc.), or create entirely new music that blends well with it. Remember also to refer back to your list of musical concepts for some ideas before you begin.

Step 6: Composing the B section

We now need to write the first contrasting musical section or **episode** of the rondo, the B section. Although **contrast** needs to be a feature of this section, we also have to maintain a sense of **unity** so that it 'fits' when played immediately after the A section. Let's consider some ways in which we can create contrast whilst still maintaining unity.

Ways of creating contrast

◆ Change **key**.

◆ Alter **rhythms**.

◆ Change **dynamic** (volume).

◆ Add new musical features/concepts (**ornaments**, **syncopation**, **staccato**, etc.).

Ways of maintaining unity

◆ Keep the musical phrases about the same length as those used in the previous section.

◆ Use a musical fragment (a bar or just a few notes) used previously, but alter it in some way (e.g. **transpose** it into the key of the new section; change a note or two; invent a new **rhythm** for it).

◆ **Repeat** the beginning of a musical phrase used previously, but complete it in a different way.

CD track 42. Below is the music of my B section, which you can hear on CD track 42, followed by a written summary of the features used in its construction.

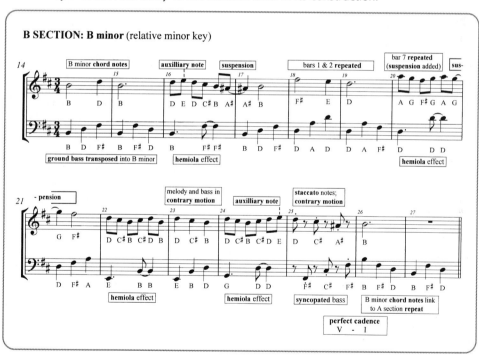

B SECTION: B minor
(relative minor key)

	Bars 14–17	Bars 18–21	Bars 22–27
Melody	First 4-bar phrase is based on 2 notes of the B minor chord (B and D), with an **auxiliary note** (E) and a **passing note** (C♯) added in bar 16. A **suspension** is used across bars 16 and 17, where the last note of bar 16 (A♯ – the **preparation** note) is held over onto beat 1 of bar 17 (creating the **suspension** note), and resolves on beat 2 onto the B (the **resolution** note).	The second 4-bar phrase is built on music already used in the A section: bars 18 and 19 are a direct **repeat** of bars 1 and 2, whereas bars 20 and 21 are a **repeat** of bars 7 and 8 but with the addition of a **suspension** – here the final G in bar 20 is held over into bar 21 to create the **suspension**, before **resolving** onto F♯ on the second beat of bar 21. This **repeat** of music from the A section creates a **passing modulation** as it changes the key briefly back into the **tonic** key of D major.	Bars 22 and 23 use two notes (B and D) from the chord of E minor 7th – the chord on which these two bars are based – as well as C♯ **passing notes**. In bar 23 we also have 3 consecutive crotchet (quarter note) beats being used for the first time in the **melodic rhythm** (these move in **contrary motion** to the three bass notes). Bar 24 is a **repeat** of bar 22 except for the last note (E), which functions as an **auxiliary** note. Bar 25 uses **staccato** notes which move in **contrary motion** to the **syncopated** bass notes. A **perfect cadence** is formed in bars 25 and 26 (V–I) to round off the B section.
Bass	Original 2-bar **ground bass** figure is **transposed** into B minor (relative minor key). In bar 16 a new **rhythm** is introduced (a dotted crotchet [dotted quarter note] followed by two tied notes) which creates a **hemiola** effect (i.e. the music briefly sounds as though the time signature has changed from 3/4 (**simple time**) to 6/8 (**compound time**).	In bars 18 and 19 the **ground bass** is **varied** again slightly, and has been raised in **pitch**. Bar 20 repeats the **hemiola** rhythm first used in bar 16.	Bars 22 and 24 **repeat** the **hemiola** rhythm; bars 23 and 25 move in **contrary motion** to the melody; and two new musical features, **syncopation** and **staccato**, are used in bar 25. Bars 26 and 27 firmly re-establish the key of B minor with the notes B, D and F♯.

Contrast in my B section

◆ Key **modulation** to B minor.

◆ The **ground bass** receives more **variation**, with the appearance of higher note **pitches** and greater variety in the **harmonic rhythm**, including **syncopation** and a dotted rhythm which creates a **hemiola** effect.

◆ **Contrary motion**, **staccato** and **suspensions** are used.

Unity in my B section

◆ The opening 8 bars of the B section use an almost identical **melodic rhythm** to that of the first 8 bars of the A section.

◆ Bar 20 is a **repeat** of bar 7 of the A section, but with a **suspension** added.

◆ The shape and flow of the quaver (eighth note) figures (**stepwise** movement with **passing notes**) is the same as in the A section.

◆ The B section has the same number of phrases as the A section (three) and, apart from the addition of one extra bar in the third phrase of the B section (bar 26), they are also four bars long.

For Practice

Keeping in mind some of the ways in which you can create *contrast* and maintain *unity*, compose the first contrasting **episode**, the B section, of your rondo now.

Step 7: The first repeat of the A section

According to strict **rondo** form, the next part involves repeating the A section. Therefore, bars 28–40 of my rondo will **repeat** bars 1–13 – but this time, to create some **variation**, I have **transposed** the melody down an **octave** and slightly altered bars 32, 34, 39 and 40 of the **ground bass** (see music below).

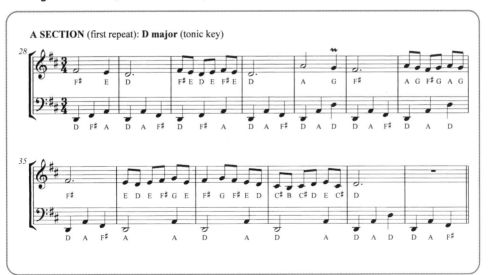

For Practice

Consider adding some **variation** to the first **repeat** of the A section in your own rondo. This may involve **transposing** the **melody** up or down an **octave**, and/or making some small alterations to either the **melody** or **ground bass**.

Step 8: Composing the C section

We are now ready to compose the second (and final) contrasting section or **episode** of the rondo, the C section. This can be approached in the same way as the B section, since both *contrast* and *unity* again need to be observed.

I have chosen to **modulate** into the key of A major (the **dominant** key) for this section of my rondo, and in addition to writing some original music (for *contrast*) I will also incorporate some of the musical fragments already used in the previous sections (for *unity*).

CD track 43. Below is the music I composed for my C section, which you can hear on CD track 43, followed by a written summary of the features used in its construction.

C SECTION: A major
(dominant key)

	Bars 41–44	Bars 45–60
Melody	A new **melody** begins in bar 41 with three **ascending stepwise** notes (C♯, D, E). These notes, and the long A note in bar 42, establish the new key of A major (A, C♯ and E are **chord notes**, and D is a **passing note**). Bar 41 also uses a dotted crotchet (dotted quarter note) as part of the **melodic rhythm** for the first time. Bar 43 **repeats** the music of bar 9 (now **transposed** down a fourth). Bar 44 introduces a new melodic idea where **descending stepwise** notes (C♯, B, A) played **on the beat**, alternate with E notes played **off the beat**. (When used in this way, the repeated note is sometimes referred to as a *pivot note*.)	The **melodic rhythm** of bars 45–48 **repeats** that of bars 41–44, but the notes are now played at a **higher pitch** (most are **transposed** up a 4th). Bar 47 is a **repeat** of bar 7. The presence of G natural in bars 45 and 47 create a **passing modulation** into D major (**tonic** key). The **ascending stepwise melody** in bar 49 (which uses a new **melodic rhythm**) is **repeated** in bars 51 and 53. Bar 50 **repeats** bar 44, but this time the pivot note (E) is **inverted** to sound an **octave** lower. Bar 52 **imitates** the **ground bass rhythm** used in bars 49 and 51. Bars 54–58 use the *pivot* technique with the notes of the **dominant chord** (E major) and the **dominant 7th chord** (E7) to create a **dominant pedal** which ends in a **perfect cadence** at bar 59 when the **tonic** chord of this section (A major) is played. Bar 60 is a **link** bar into the final **repeat** of the A section: the G natural in the **ground bass** here helps to **modulate** the music back to the **tonic** key (D major) again, whilst the C♯ will rise comfortably onto the D note which follows in the next bar.
Bass	2-bar **ground bass** figure **transposed** into A major (the **dominant** key).	In bars 41–44 the **ground bass** plays the **chord notes** of A major, and in bars 45–49 the **chord notes** of D major. Bar 47 creates the rhythmic effect of a **hemiola** again (first used in the B section). The **rhythm** of bars 49–53 is more **varied** than anywhere else in the rondo, causing the **ground bass** to sound more like a harmonic **counterpoint** here. The steady **rhythm** of the **ground bass** returns at bar 54 and continues to the end of the piece.

Contrast in my C section

◆ Key **modulation** to A major (the **dominant** key).

◆ This is the longest section in the rondo (20 bars in total) and the phrase structure is also different: there are four phrases (bars 41–44, 45–48, 49–52 and 53–60), each four bars in length except for the last (53–60) which is eight bars long – the **dominant pedal** used in bars 55–58 helps to extend this phrase.

◆ **Leaping melodies** as well as **stepwise melodies** are now used.

◆ A new musical technique is introduced in bar 44 where the melody alternates with a single repeating E note (sometimes referred to as a 'pivot' note because the music constantly pivots back and forth between it and the main melody notes).

◆ In bars 49–53 the **rhythm** of the **ground bass** is more **varied**, creating a **contrapuntal** texture here.

Unity in my C section

◆ Both **melody** and **ground bass** parts **repeat** individual bars and rhythms used previously in each of the other sections.

◆ The combination of original music and previously used material helps to make this section sound like a small **development** of all the musical elements which have gone into making the rondo.

For Practice

Start composing the C section of your rondo now, keeping *contrast* and *unity* in mind just as you did when working on the B section. You might choose to keep the new section the same length as the others, but composers often make this **episode** of the rondo a longer one in which they **develop** the material of the previous sections.

Step 9: The final repeat of the A section

To complete the rondo, all that is required now is one last **repeat** of the A section at its original **pitch**, but I am also going to add a short **Coda** in order to conclude the piece more decisively.

I wanted the **Coda** to be brief but interesting, so I finally decided that a short *flourish* of notes beginning half way through the last phrase of the section (bar 70), and ending on the key note D (bar 72), would work well. To that I added another two bars (to extend the phrase a little more), the second of which contains the key note again but played **staccato** this time and an **octave** higher than the previous key note in bar 72. This has the effect of concluding my rondo in a decisive and light-hearted way.

CD track 44. The music for the final **repeat** of my A section, complete with short **Coda**, is shown on the following page. You can hear it on CD track 44.

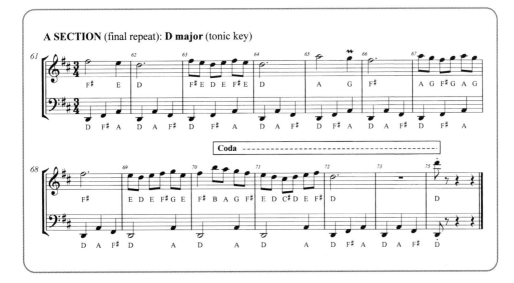

A SECTION (final repeat): **D major** (tonic key)

For Practice

Play your own A section a few times again to try to work out what sort of music will make an effective **Coda** (if you want to have one) for your rondo. Will it be a rapid flourish of notes, or perhaps an **ascending** (or **descending**) passage which moves steadily towards the key note? Or maybe you have something else in mind? Take your time and experiment with different ideas before composing your **Coda**, and remember that it need only be about 2–6 bars in length.

Step 10: Composing the chord accompaniment

Now that the **melody** and **ground bass** have been composed, we just need to add the third (or middle) part, the chord accompaniment, and the rondo will be complete.

The good news is that this will be the easiest part to write because we have already had to think about **chords** when selecting the notes for the **ground bass** (and therefore the **harmony** for each bar has been established), and also because the **rhythm** of the chord accompaniment will need to be fairly simple since anything that is too 'busy' could interfere with the other two parts. Focusing on *longer note values* will help to ensure that the accompaniment isn't too obtrusive, as will the use of **rests**. In addition to using straightforward **root position** chords, we can also experiment with the sounds of different **chord inversions** in this accompaniment part.

CD track 45. On the following page you will find the full score of my finished rondo (which I decided to name *'Dance Rondo'* because of its lively **triple metre**), complete with chord accompaniment. You can hear the music on CD track 45. Notice that, although I have kept the accompaniment fairly simple, it still has enough rhythmic variety to make it both interesting and different from the other parts. Notice also how I have made use of **chord inversions** and added some **dynamics** for 'colour'.

For Practice

Using the notes of your **ground bass** as a guide, choose **chords** to accompany each bar of your rondo and then compose a simple **rhythm** (or rhythms) for these chords. Again, a good way to experiment with the chords and rhythms for this task will be to try out various ideas while the other two parts of your rondo are being played back to you (either by other musicians or using a keyboard or MIDI sequencer).

Dance Rondo

Joe McGowan

Extension Ideas

Here are some ideas you could use should you wish to extend and **develop** your rondo even more.

◆ **Repeat** each section (perhaps adding some **variation** in these repeats).

◆ Compose a second melody (a fourth part), to be played by another **solo** instrument. This would give you the opportunity to use features such as **imitation** (where the two solo instruments repeat each other's music like an 'echo'), **unisons** and harmonic **intervals** of a *third*, a *sixth* and an *octave*, as well as **counterpoint**. You might also have these two solo instruments *alternate* with each other by playing a section each (*solo*) before playing the final A section (*together*) in **unison**.

◆ Vary the **dynamics** more (perhaps adding **crescendos** and **diminuendos**).

◆ Include **tempo** variations, such as ritardando (***rit.***) and accelerando (***accel.***).

◆ Add **articulation** to the **solo** part(s) such as **staccato**, **legato**, **slurs**, **accents**.

◆ Write a longer **Coda**, taking care that it sounds balanced with the rest of the piece.

◆ **Repeat** the music of the B section again after the second repeat of the A section, but this time **transpose** it into the **tonic** key – doing this will also mean that you can add yet another repeat of the A section. Notice the new symmetry of a rondo with that structure:

A	B	A	C	A	B	A
Tonic key	Relative minor key, Subdominant key (IV), or Dominant key	Tonic key	Relative minor key, Subdominant key (IV), or Dominant key	Tonic key	Tonic key	Tonic key

Summary of the Compositional Processes and Techniques used in 'Dance Rondo'

In this workshop you followed certain steps to compose a sizeable and well structured piece of music. These steps, which are summarised below, can be followed when you write any new piece of music.

◆ Make a note of the basic musical elements or concepts (e.g. *style*, *structure*, *tempo*, *key*, etc.) that will form the basis of your piece.

◆ Sketch a structure plan – doing this at the start means you will have something to refer to which will keep you on the right track as you compose, and also ensure that your piece will have a balanced structure when it is complete.

◆ Begin simply by composing just the first phrase or so of the piece (we began the rondo by writing the 2-bar **ground bass**, followed by the first 4 bars of the **melody**).

◆ Explore ways in which you can **develop** more music from that first phrase using techniques (or concepts) like **melodic** and **harmonic sequence**, **passing notes**, **variation**, **repetition**, **retrograde**, **inversion**, **syncopation** and so on.

◆ Work in small sections, composing just a few bars or phrases at a time as you build up the piece.

◆ Always keep in mind ways to create **contrast** and maintain **unity** in your piece, such as mixing original bars of music with bars that have been used before, or **repeating** musical **rhythms** that have been used before but with different notes.

◆ Swapping around the order of note passages and bars can create both **contrast** and **unity**. For example, you might take a 4-bar phrase from an earlier section of the piece and play it in **retrograde** (backwards) or in **inversion** (as a mirror image of itself), or 'jumble up' the order of the bars any way you choose – if it sounds good, it works!

◆ Take a phrase or a passage of music from one part (e.g. the main melody) and **repeat** it in a different part (e.g. the bass) at a different **pitch**.

◆ Re-using musical ideas and phrases throughout your piece, whether **repeating** these exactly or with some **variation**, not only uses the *minimum* of musical material to *maximum* effect, but also helps to create **contrast** whilst maintaining **unity**.

Making a Programme Note for Your Rondo

A requirement for Higher Music is that each composition or arrangement in your folio should be accompanied by a programme note detailing the processes involved in the creation of the work. Below is an example of a programme note that could be prepared for 'Dance Rondo'.

Programme Note	'Dance Rondo'	by Joe McGowan

Stimulus
I wanted to compose a piece of instrumental music which incorporates some of the musical concepts I have been studying in Higher Music. The instrumental dances of the renaissance and baroque periods interested me so I decided to write a lively work in rondo form with a ground bass.

Resources
Piano, violin, manuscript paper and MIDI keyboard linked to a computer running a MIDI sequencer.

Significant Decisions
I wanted to write a rondo that could be performed either as a trio or a piano and violin duet (mainly because these are two instruments I play myself). The ground bass and chord parts of my rondo can be played on two separate instruments or piano (one part for each hand), whilst the melody is suited to an instrument (such as the violin) capable of sustaining notes in a lyrical way.

Use of technology
MIDI keyboard and sequencer, which involved using many of the sequencer's functions such as Loop, Arrange, Quantise, Edit and Transpose to make an arrangement of *Dance Rondo* which I printed, saved as a MIDI file and burned onto CD.

Use of improvisation
I improvised with scales in various keys over the ground bass (played back in a loop using the sequencer) in order to compose the basic melodic ideas for each section of the rondo.

Audio Recording Arrangements
In addition to the MIDI recording, I also produced a live recording of *Dance Rondo* on which I perform the melody on violin accompanied by my teacher playing the chord and ground bass parts on piano (this is my duet arrangement of the piece).

Process
I began by making a list of all the things I wanted to include in this piece (ground bass, ornaments, suspensions, passing notes, etc.), as well as writing a structure plan. I composed a basic two-bar ground bass figure first, which is repeated with occasional variation throughout the rondo. I then wrote the first 4-bar phrase of the melody, developing and re-using this basic material all through the piece as well as experimenting/improvising in the keys of D major, B minor and A major to create the main sections of my rondo (which modulate into different keys). I also experimented with intervals of a third, a sixth and an octave to help me produce good harmony with the ground bass. Last of all I composed the middle part, the chord accompaniment, using the melody and ground bass as a guide to chord choice.

Workshop 3: Composing 'Scots Song'

This composing workshop focuses on a vocal piece which will get its 'Scottish sound' from the use of **modal** music (often used in songs and ballads of this type).

Although I will not be adding lyrics to the piece written in the workshop (I'm leaving this as an optional practice exercise for you!), you should of course do so in your own song, either when the melody is completed or while you are composing it.

Alternatively, you might choose to compose music to fit existing words – which could be your own. But just remember, should you write lyrics to the song I have composed for this workshop and end up with a recording deal… we split the royalties!

We will begin by composing the **melody** one step at a time, paying attention to particular musical elements (concepts) which can provide the piece with its Scottish character, and then add a piano accompaniment. The finished song for solo voice and piano will then be **arranged** as an instrumental piece using a MIDI sequencer (page 88–90).

Before we start composing, let's review **modal** music.

The seven basic modes

Modes date back to medieval times before music notation as we know it today was developed. Although the names of the modes can sound a bit complex, modal music is actually very simple to understand.

This mode...	begins on this note...
Ionian	C
Dorian	D
Phrygian	E
Lydian	F
Mixolydian	G
Aeolian	A
Locrian	B

If you choose a D note on a keyboard instrument and then play only the successive *white keys* up (or down) to the next D (one **octave**), this is the *Dorian* mode. Do the same thing starting on an F and you will play the *Lydian* mode. It's that simple! Every modal scale has a unique sound because a different order of **tones** and **semitones** occurs in each **mode**.

The starting note of a **mode** can be considered the 'home' note to which, much like a key note in **tonal** music, you would return whenever you wanted to create a phrase ending – as in a **perfect cadence**.

Hints and Tips

To help you remember the order of the modes (beginning with C), you might find the following phrase a useful memory-jogger:

I	Don't	Pretend	Little	Monkeys	Are	Large!
O	O	H	Y	I	E	O
N	R	R	D	X	O	C
I	I	Y	I	O	L	R
A	A	G	A	L	I	I
N	N	I	N	Y	A	A
		A		D	N	N
		N		I		
				A		
				N		

Chords built from modal scales

Since the order of **tones** and **semitones** changes in each **modal** scale, it follows that the ordering of chords (whether **major** or **minor**) built from the notes in these scales will also vary. For example, the chord built from the first note of the *Ionian* mode (C) is C major, whereas in the *Dorian* mode (beginning on D) the first chord is D *minor*.

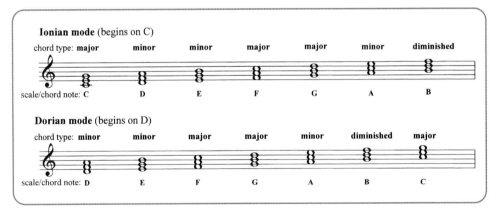

Important points about modal music

♦ No key signatures are used in the seven *basic* modes, but **accidentals** (sharps and flats) can be used to add 'colour' or **chromaticism** in a piece of **modal** music, and at **cadences** where the 7th note of the **mode** is often sharpened to create a smooth **perfect cadence**.

♦ **Harmony** is generally much simpler in **modal** music than it is in **tonal** music, with less variety of **chords** and fewer chord **inversions** used. This helps to maintain the simplicity and specific character of the modal sound.

♦ The **chords** chosen to harmonise a **modal** melody can greatly strengthen the modal sound. For example, the chords built from the *second* and *third* notes of a modal scale are often used freely for their particular sound. In **tonal** music these chords (II and III) are generally used less frequently, and often appear as part of a specific chord progression such as **II–V–I** (D minor – G major – C major, for example).

◆ Other types of modes known as 'altered modes' exist. These are modes which have certain notes altered to make specific sounds, and are most commonly used in modern popular styles such as rock music.

Using keys with modal music

Modes can also be used in music which has a key. If you think of each mode as representing the seven different notes of a scale, you can easily play any **mode** in any *key*.

For example, consider that the modes are numbered from 1 to 7:

1 **Ionian**

2 **Dorian**

3 **Phrygian**

4 **Lydian**

5 **Mixolydian**

6 **Aeolian**

7 **Locrian**

The number of each mode corresponds to the same note number of a scale. So, if you are in the key of B flat major and choose the *fourth* note of that scale (E flat) as your 'key note' instead of B flat, you will create the *Lydian* mode. Choose the third note of the same scale (D) as the key note and you will now get the *Phrygian* mode.

For Practice

Try experimenting with the sounds of different modes in a variety of keys. First select a key, then work your way up through the modes from Ionian to Locrian, choosing each note of the scale (1–7) as a new 'key note'.

Step 1: The plan for 'Scots Song'

When composing most types of songs, you either write music to existing lyrics (which you may have also written yourself), or compose the music first and then choose lyrics to suit the notes and **rhythm**. Sometimes it can be a combination of both methods, and the piece will grow from a number of musical and lyrical ideas. In my Scots song I am going to concentrate on the melody first, and leave the lyrics to *you*!

To add a little more interest to my song, I have chosen not to take the more traditional approach of writing clearly defined **verse** and **chorus** (or **refrain**) sections (although you can do so if you wish), but instead base the song on three different melodic ideas – or **themes** as I will be calling them. The themes will **contrast** slightly with each other but still be related through certain common **rhythms** and note patterns, with parts being **repeated**, sometimes with **variation**, throughout the piece. The aim of this type of plan is to produce a less formal or 'looser' structure which sounds more **through-composed** than would be the case had I chosen a **verse-chorus-verse** formula.

If you have worked through the first composing workshop you should be familiar with some of the helpful processes composers often use to write a new piece of music. To begin, remember that it is very helpful to jot down all your ideas – including the musical elements or concepts you think will help to create the right style and mood – followed by a basic structure plan. You don't need to stick rigidly to this plan, of course, but even working loosely within a certain structure can ensure that your final piece will be well-balanced.

Here are my own ideas and structure plan:

Elements which will help to create a 'Scottish' sound

◆ **Scotch snaps**

◆ **Dotted rhythms**

◆ **Modal** and/or **pentatonic** scales

◆ Fairly simple **chords/harmony** (with chords II and III used for their **modal** sound)

◆ Instruments: **voice** with **piano accompaniment** (which could be extended or arranged to include folk instruments such as **fiddle**, **whistle**, **clarsach** and **guitar**)

Other useful elements

◆ **4-bar piano introduction**

◆ **Through-composed** or 'loose' structure

◆ Recurring melodic **theme** (functioning as a kind of **chorus** or **refrain**)

◆ **Instrumental** section

◆ Simple but memorable musical phrases

◆ **Anacrusis**

Structure Plan

SECTION	A	B	A 1
4-bar piano introduction	Theme 1 Ionian mode 'Major' sound (use major chords)	Theme 2 (contrast) 'Minor' sound (add minor chords)	First repeat of Theme 1 with some slight variation
4 bars	4–8 bars	4–8 bars	4–8 bars

C	A 2	D	A 3
Theme 3 (change mode for contrast) 'Minor' sound (use different minor chords from those used in Theme 2)	Second repeat of Theme 1 with a new kind of variation	Piano Instrumental based on section C (Theme 3) or previously-heard melodic fragments	Coda Consisting of a final varied repeat of Theme 1, perhaps with a metre change
4–8 bars	4–8 bars	4–8 bars	4–8 bars

Notice the similarity between the planned structure for my song and **rondo** form. Most songs have a kind of rondo structure where the **chorus** can be regarded as the recurring 'A' section and the **verses** the contrasting **episodes** (B, C and D sections).

For Practice

Start off your own Scots song now by making a list of the musical elements or concepts that you think will be effective in your piece, followed by a structure plan sketch. When working out your plan, remember that songs and ballads normally have **verses** (where the lyrics change with each new verse) and **refrains** or **choruses** (where the lyrics are normally the same each time), but you can also choose a more loose structure as I have. Before you begin work on your song it would be helpful to listen to a few Scottish songs/ballads for some inspiration and structural guidelines.

Step 2: Composing Section A (Theme 1)

Although I want to begin my song with a 4-bar piano introduction, I will not write this until the rest of the piece has been composed, since the completed song will help to determine the music of the introduction.

The style of this piece dictates that the music should be kept fairly simple, with no overly-complicated vocal passages or complex accompaniment, but that doesn't mean we can't write a really good, atmospheric and memorable melody – the kind you might find yourself whistling or humming spontaneously while walking down the street! So the aim is to make each note matter, whilst keeping everything reasonably uncomplicated.

A comfortable vocal **range** is from about middle C to the C an **octave** above it.

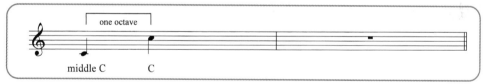

Of course, it is possible to sing notes much higher and lower than this, depending on the skill of the singer and whether the voice is male or female (I have a **soprano** voice in mind for my song, so I can go a bit higher), but keeping within a certain **range** means that more people will be able to sing the music you compose.

I have chosen to build my song from the basic **Ionian mode**, beginning on the note C. Written below are the seven main **chords** of this mode; these will help me to compose the song since I can use **chord notes** to construct parts of my melody, or let the sound of certain chord progressions influence each new **theme** I write.

Chords in the Ionian mode

Mode note	C	D	E	F	G	A	B
Chord	C Major	D Minor	E Minor	F Major	G Major	A Minor	B Diminished
	(I)	(II)	(III)	(IV)	(V)	(VI)	(VII)

You will see that the notes and chords of the Ionian mode are the same as those found in the key of C major. That is because in each case there are no sharps or flats (accidentals) used. In all other modes the difference in the sound is more obvious. For example, the basic Dorian mode (which would begin on the second note (D) in the above example) doesn't have the F♯ and C♯ found in the key of *D major*, or the B♭ and C♯ found in the key of *D minor*.

I had no melodic ideas in my head for the song when I began, so in order to try to generate something, I started improvising/experimenting with the *Ionian mode* and the *C pentatonic major scale* (the notes of which are also found in the Ionian mode), as well as various **chord notes**, whilst incorporating **dotted rhythms** and **Scotch snaps**. I soon came up with a 4-bar phrase I liked (note the **chords** written above the music which helped to influence the **melody** notes).

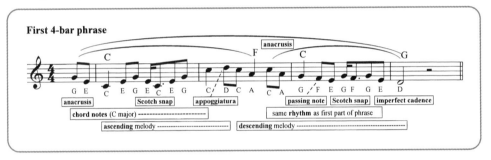

CD Track 46. You can hear this opening phrase on CD track 46.

The 4-bar phrase is made up of two smaller phrases (indicated by the two phrase marks underneath the longer single phrase mark) which have an almost identical **rhythm** and use **anacrusis** and **Scotch snaps** (notice also how this opening phrase makes use of **chord notes** and a single **appoggiatura** and **passing note**). The full phrase finishes on the note D, forming an **imperfect cadence** (had I wanted to end more decisively I could have chosen a note here that would fit with the chord of C in order to make a **perfect cadence**).

All of the elements used for this opening phrase are going to be important in the construction of the rest of the song.

The effect of the **imperfect cadence** at the end of my first phrase has been to create a **Question** which needs an **Answer** to balance it out and so complete a larger section of music. This section will be the first **theme** of my song as outlined in the structure plan.

Having already established the song's character and central musical elements in the opening 4-bar **Question** phrase, I used these to guide me as I wrote the **Answer** phrase – the natural flow of which seemed to move down towards the note C and a **perfect cadence**.

CD Track 47. The **Question** and **Answer** phrases which make up **Theme 1** of my song are shown on the following page; follow the notation as you listen to the music on CD track 47.

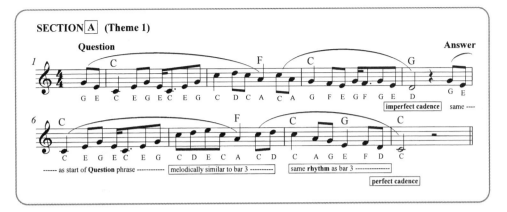

SECTION A (Theme 1)

Features of *contrast* in the *Answer* phrase

◆ Bars 7, 8 and 9 are original music.

◆ The **Answer** phrase ends with a **perfect cadence** in bar 9.

Features of *unity* in the *Question* and *Answer* phrases

◆ The first part of the **Answer** phrase (end of bar 5 and all of bar 6) is the same as the start of the **Question** phrase (end of bar 1 and all of bar 2).

◆ The second full bar of the **Answer** phrase (bar 7) has some **melodic** similarity to the second full bar of the **Question** phrase (bar 3).

For Practice

Following the plan for your own Scots song (and using my opening **theme** as a guide), compose a melodic **theme** or a **verse** which has a strong Scottish feel to it, bearing in mind the musical elements which can help you to achieve this, such as **Scotch snaps**, **dotted rhythms** and **modal** or **pentatonic** scales. Just start experimenting and see what kind of 'tunes' begin to develop!

Once you have completed the music of your opening **verse** or **theme** you might want to **repeat** it (perhaps with some **variation**) and make this extended melody the first section of your song. Doing that would of course expand your finished piece further, but remember, the most important thing is that the music 'feels' right when you hear it, so always let your instinct guide you.

Step 3: Composing Section B (Theme 2)

If you worked on the **rondo** in the first composing workshop, you will be practised in how to create **contrast** whilst preserving **unity** in a piece of music (look back over this workshop to refresh your memory if necessary).

For **contrast** in my second theme I am going to raise the **pitch** of the notes a little, and also create a slightly darker sound in places by using melody notes taken from minor chords found in the Ionian mode. To maintain a sense of **unity** I will include **Scotch snaps** and **anacrusis**, and keep the same kind of 2-bar phrase structure used in the first theme.

ARRANGING AND COMPOSING

Here are the various points I noted down before composing the second theme:

Contrast:

◆ Create a darker sound by building parts of the melody from **minor** chords used in the Ionian mode.

◆ Raise the **pitch** of the melody slightly.

Unity:

◆ Keep using **Scotch snaps**.

◆ Keep using **anacrusis**.

◆ Add some fragments of the melody used in the first theme, but **vary** these – perhaps by **inverting** note groups.

CD Track 48. Below is the music of my second theme which you can hear on CD track 48. Note the **chords** (written above the music) which helped to influence the **melody**.

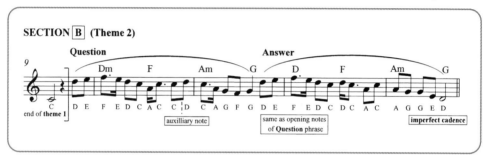

You will see that the second theme is just four bars long. The single 4-bar phrase sounded effective when played after the music of the first theme, so I was happy to make this alteration to the 4-bar **Question** phrase / 4-bar **Answer** phrase structure of Theme 1 – which in itself provides an element of **variation**. The second theme still has **Question** and **Answer** phrases, but these are each just two bars long instead of four.

According to plan, though, I have raised the **pitch** of the **melody** and added some 'darker' minor chords for **contrast** whilst maintaining **unity** through the **rhythm**, **Scotch snaps** and **anacrusis**. Notice also how I have incorporated **passing notes** and an **auxiliary note** between the **chord notes**.

The second theme ends on the note D (from the chord of G major), making an **imperfect cadence** which will lead the music nicely into the first **repeat** of Theme 1.

For Practice

Write the next part of your song now (which in your case might be a **chorus/refrain**, or a new **theme**), keeping in mind the techniques I have just used in my own piece to create both **contrast** and **unity** whilst still preserving the basic simplicity of the melody.

Step 4: Composing Section A1 (Theme 1 repeated with some variation)

The next part of the structure plan for my song involves **repeating** Theme 1 with a little **variation** added to it. Here are some variation techniques which might be used in a repeated section of music:

◆ Add some new **melodic** material in between bars of **repeated** music.

◆ Change one or two notes in a bar.

◆ Create a new **rhythm** for parts of the **repeated** music.

◆ Create a new **melody** for a **rhythm** which is being **repeated**.

◆ Reduce/increase the length of the repeated section.

CD Track 49. Here is my music for the varied repeat of Theme 1, which you can hear on CD track 49. Compare it with the original version of Theme 1 on page 77 (CD track 47).

You will see that again I have used just a single 4-bar phrase for this section, shortening the **repeat** of the first theme by half and finishing with a **perfect cadence**. I have also rearranged the music so that the notes now fall on *different beats of the bar* to those of the original first theme; the **anacrusis** at the start of the repeat of Theme 1, for example, now begins on beat *two* of the bar as opposed to beat *four* – this 'displaces' all the beats of the music which follows. You might think that doing this would have upset the overall symmetry of the piece, but in fact the result is quite effective, and has produced a nice element of **variation**.

Also for **variation** I reversed the order of the opening **anacrusis** notes and inserted some new melodic material in bars 15, 16 and 17, while a sense of **unity** is maintained through the **repetition** of certain notes and **rhythms** from the original Theme 1.

For Practice

Depending on the structure you have chosen for your Scots song, at this stage you will be either repeating the first **theme** (like me) or writing a second **verse** (this could be a varied **repeat** of your first **verse**). If you are repeating Theme 1, consider the possibility of adding some **variation** (which may simply involve reducing the length of the section), but you may ultimately feel that an *identical* repeat is the preferable option. Whatever the case, the last three composing steps will be a helpful guide to you.

Step 5: Composing Section C (Theme 3)

Now it's time to write the next section of new music for my song, the third **theme**. As before, the main aim will be to create **contrast** here for melodic interest whilst still preserving the basic **unity**, simplicity and flow overall.

Here is the list of ideas I had for achieving both **contrast** and **unity** in the new theme:

Contrast:

◆ Base the new theme on the **Aeolian mode** (minor sound), but return to the original **Ionian mode** (major sound) again at the end since the next section (the second repeat of Theme 1) will be in this mode.

◆ Add some new **rhythms**.

◆ Alter the **rhythm** of the **anacrusis**.

Unity:

◆ Maintain the same basic rhythmic flow and phrase structure as the previous sections of music.

◆ Keep using **Scotch snaps**.

◆ Use some rhythms/melodic fragments from previous sections of the piece.

To spark off some ideas for this new **theme** I tried **improvising** with the *Aeolian mode*, the *A pentatonic minor scale* (the notes of which are also found in the Aeolian mode) and the **chord notes** of A minor and E minor (chords I and V of the Aeolian mode), whilst also incorporating my ideas for achieving **contrast** and **unity**.

CD Track 50. Working within these helpful and structured guidelines it wasn't long before I had composed my new theme (shown at the top of the following page). Study the music carefully now before listening to it on CD track 50, noting the ways in which I have made use of the following:

◆ **Chord notes**

◆ **Passing notes**

◆ Aeolian mode/A pentatonic minor

◆ New **rhythms**: dotted crotchets (dotted quarter notes) and semiquavers (sixteenth notes)

◆ **Repeated rhythms**

◆ **Repeated** bars and note groups

◆ **Variation**

◆ **Scotch snaps**

◆ New **anacrusis** rhythm

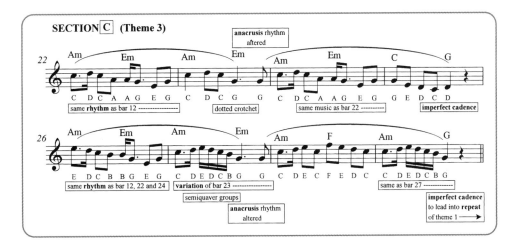

SECTION C (Theme 3)

For Practice

If you are writing your song with a traditional **verse-chorus-verse** structure, the next step for you will probably involve **repeating** the **chorus** you have already composed. If, on the other hand, you are following *my* structure you now need to write a third contrasting **theme**, perhaps changing the **scale** or **mode** in order to create a **modulation**. Remember that by adding just a single new **rhythm** you can inject an element of **variation** into your music.

Step 6: Section A2 (second repeat of Theme 1)

After playing all of the sections I had composed so far (in order), now seemed the right time to **repeat** all eight bars of Theme 1 (as opposed to reducing it to just four bars as I did in the first repeat of the theme at bar 14). I made just two small changes to the theme this time (see music below): the first was to add three new notes in bar 36 (the high F note adds a bit more drama as well as **variation**), the second involved tagging on an extra bar in **2/4 time** at the end. The 2/4 bar is used to extend the end of the theme and create a little extra 'breathing space' before the next section, the *piano instrumental*, begins. Doing this also strengthens the suggestion that one section of music has finished and another new one is about to start.

CD Track 51. Listen to the second repeat of Theme 1 on CD track 51 now while you follow the music below.

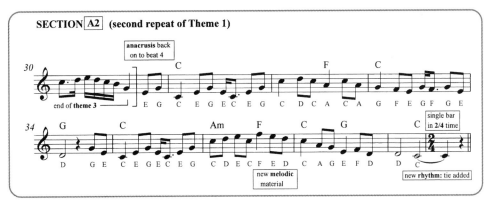

SECTION A2 (second repeat of Theme 1)

81

For Practice

Your own song will probably be repeating a **theme** or a **verse** now, in which you might want to add some small (but effective) **variations** as I did in the second **repeat** of my first theme. The simple addition of an extra bar to create a smooth **link** into the next section of your piece might be all that's needed, or you could decide to do something a bit more creative, such as **modulate** into another mode or add some completely new **rhythms**. You might feel, however, that the best result will be achieved by simply **repeating** a previous **theme/verse** with no variation at all. Don't be tempted to add something different to your piece just for the sake of doing so; often the most straightforward option will produce the best musical effect, so don't try to be *too* clever!

Step 7: Section D (the piano instrumental)

Although the main role of the piano in my song is to provide an **accompaniment** (composed later in this workshop), in the **instrumental** section its function will also be **melodic**, where it will **repeat** the **melody** of Theme 3 (with the right hand), and accompany itself using **chords** (played by the left hand). Having an instrument **repeat** a phrase or a whole section of music which was previously sung (or played on a different instrument) is another effective composing technique which provides both **contrast** and **unity** – without the need to write any new material!

Since the piano will be simply **repeating** Theme 3 without any **variation**, there is no need to give a musical example here, but you will see how this section (complete with **chord** accompaniment) fits alongside the rest of the music when the notation for the completed song is given on page 84.

For Practice

If the plan for your Scots song includes an instrumental section, consider following my example by **repeating** music which was previously written for the vocal part, such as a **verse**, **theme** or **chorus**. Alternatively you could compose an instrumental which incorporates only *fragments* of the vocal melody used in other parts of the piece, or even write a completely original section of music.

Step 8: Composing Section A3 (Coda – varied repeat of Theme 1)

To finish my **melody** I have chosen to write a **Coda** based on a **variation** of Theme 1. However, if the ending is to stand out from the previous music, this time the **variation** technique will have to be different from any I have used so far.

In my structure plan I noted the possibility of changing the **metre** of the music here, which would mean that I could vary the original theme considerably without having to alter the **pitch** of any of the notes. The first contrasting metre which came to mind was **triple metre**, so I tried playing Theme 1 in **3/4 time**, changing some of the **rhythms** and using **augmentation** in places where this felt right, and was pleased with the result straight away. The change of metre, combined with **augmentation**, had the effect of slowing down the melody a little without there actually being a reduction in **tempo**. This was a particularly effective kind of **variation** to have in my **Coda** – again achieved using composing techniques which allowed me to produce something new without actually having to write a whole new section of music.

CD Track 52. Listen to my **Coda** on CD track 52 now whilst following the music below. Afterwards, note the elements of **contrast** and **unity** I incorporated into this final section of my Scots song.

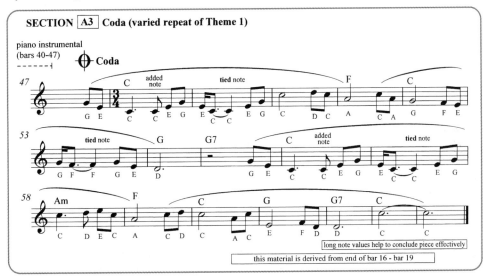

Contrast:

◆ **Metre change** to **3/4 time**, meaning that most of the notes from Theme 1 now play on a different beat of the bar than previously. (Theme 1 was originally in **4/4 time**.)

◆ **Augmentation** used on some of the notes to increase their values: dotted crotchets (dotted quarter notes), **ties** and minims (half notes) are used for this purpose.

◆ An extra note is added in bar 48, and again in bar 56.

Unity:

◆ The **Coda repeats** most of the **melody** of Theme 1, with only the last few bars altered to conclude the piece more emphatically.

For Practice

For this final step in your song's melody you might be **repeating** the **chorus/refrain** with little or no **variation**, or you could make the last section an extended **Coda** as I have in order to create a more notable ending. Think it over carefully, drawing upon the various ideas and techniques used so far in this workshop to guide you as you consider the options for making your ending a little different. As always, experiment and remember to trust your instincts concerning what sounds good, as opposed to doing something clever just for its own sake.

CD track 53. Here is the completed **melody** of my Scots song showing the **chords** which helped to influence its construction and which will also be used to **harmonise** it when I write the piano accompaniment in step 9. Follow the music notation of the song as you listen to it on CD track 53.

Step 9: The piano accompaniment

As the **chords** that I will be using to compose the piano accompaniment are the same as those which helped me write the **melody**, all I really need to do now is think about *how* I am going to use these chords again to write a good accompaniment.

The relative simplicity of the song means that I don't want to write a complex piano part that will either interfere too much with the natural flow of the **melody** or conflict with the style of the music in general.

For Practice

If you haven't already decided upon the **chords** you will be using to **harmonise** your song in the piano accompaniment, do this now. Experiment with all the chords in the **mode**(s) you have used, but keep the accompaniment uncomplicated – and don't forget that chords II and III can be incorporated freely in **modal** harmony.

When I was experimenting with different accompaniment styles and **chord inversions** it became obvious that the more basic styles were indeed the most effective, and anything which was too busy (or clever!) could easily disturb the all-important flow of the **melody**. Even those chords which contained more than the three notes of a basic **triad** often sounded a little too powerful, so I eventually settled for a straightforward but effective piano accompaniment style where the right hand plays the **triad** and the left hand has a single-note **bass** line. (The bass line determines the *position* of each chord: *root position*, *first inversion* or *second inversion*. See entry for **Inversion** in the musical concept glossary, page 126.) This style ensures that the **harmony** is well established in every bar but none of the **chords** are overpowering and the accompaniment in general is uncomplicated.

I also wanted to avoid having similar **rhythms** between the **melody** and piano accompaniment so, in addition to keeping the accompaniment simple, I introduced a dotted crotchet and quaver (dotted quarter note and eighth note) rhythm into this part, which provided **contrast** with the upper melody without interfering with it.

CD Track 54. Shown on the following page are the first five bars of the melody of 'Scots Song', complete with piano accompaniment, which you can hear on CD track 54 (you will see the full version on pages 88–90, CD track 56). I have used chord **inversions** in the accompaniment both to add interest to bars where the same chord is used throughout, and to prevent the bass line from sounding too static.

Roman numerals (I, II, IV, V) describe the chord used, where I is C major, II is D minor and so on. A **first inversion** chord is indicated by a Roman numeral followed by the letter 'b' (Ib to describe a **first inversion** of the C major chord, for example), and **V7** is used to describe the **dominant seventh chord**.

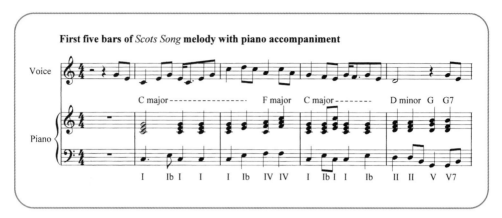

First five bars of *Scots Song* **melody with piano accompaniment**

There are two places in my song where I alter this style of accompaniment: the *piano instrumental* section and the **Coda**. In the piano instrumental you will remember that the right hand plays the **melody**, so I had to 'switch' the **chords** from right hand to left hand here, and in the **Coda** I have *both* hands playing chords in certain places; this adds power to the section and helps reinforce the effect of the music reaching its conclusion.

Other features of my piano accompaniment include **passing notes** and **contrary motion**, and there are one or two areas where the bass part (left hand) *answers* the melody or *imitates* a **melodic rhythm** used earlier in the piece. All of these features in the accompaniment can be seen on the score of 'Scots Song' which is given on pages 88–90.

Step 10: The piano introduction

To complete my Scots song all I have to do now is write the 4-bar piano **introduction**.

As I predicted in the early stages of this workshop, leaving the introduction to last made the task easier since I was able to draw upon various musical features already used in the piece to compose an Introduction which sounded balanced with the rest of the music.

I based the 4-bar piano Introduction on a straightforward **descending** phrase which uses **anacrusis**, **Scotch snap** and dotted crotchet notes (dotted quarter notes) in its construction, as well as simple **triads** in the left hand part.

CD Track 55. You can hear the piano **Introduction** on CD track 55, the music of which is shown on the following page.

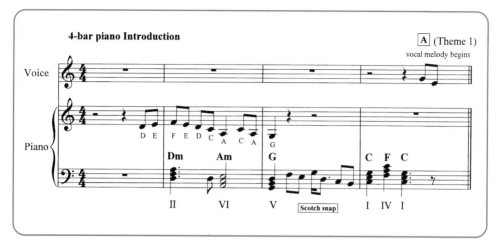

4-bar piano Introduction

A (Theme 1)

vocal melody begins

Voice

Piano

D E F E D C A C A G

Dm **Am** **G** **C F C**

II VI V Scotch snap I IV I

CD Track 56. Now listen to 'Scots Song' in its entirety, complete with piano accompaniment, on CD track 56. The musical score of the piece is printed on pages 88–90, followed by a structure summary on page 91.

A **second inversion chord** is indicated by the letter 'c' after the Roman numeral describing the chord used (for example, **IVc** means a *second inversion* of the *subdominant* chord, F major). The symbol **V7d** indicates the **dominant seventh chord** with the 'seventh' note used as the bass note – in this case F, the 'seventh' in a **G7** chord. This is known as a **third inversion** chord.

For Practice

After listening to 'Scots Song' and carefully studying the score, complete your own song by writing a piano accompaniment for it, including an **Introduction** (if you want to have one). Use my piano accompaniment as a guide to aspects such as **style**, **chord inversions**, **contrary motion**, **variation** techniques and so on, and to give you some ideas which you may want to **develop** even further (just remember not to make the accompaniment so busy that it begins to drown out your **melody**). An effective method is to **harmonise** the **melody** first of all using just a single **chord** in each bar, then experiment with various **rhythms**, **chord inversions**, **passing notes** and so on, listening to what sounds good as you gradually **develop** the accompaniment a little at a time.

ARRANGING AND COMPOSING

Scots Song Structure Summary

'Scots Song' Structure Summary	
Introduction Bars 1–4	**A** **(Theme 1)** Ionian mode – 'major' sound. End of bar 4 – bar 12
One 4-bar phrase based on a **descending** melody containing **dotted crotchet** (dotted quarter note) **rhythms** and a **Scotch snap**.	Two 4-bar phrases. First phrase introduces the central **rhythms** and mood of the piece, ending with an **imperfect cadence** (bar 8). Second phrase (end of bar 8 – bar 12) **repeats** much of the material of the first phrase with some **variation** added, and ends with a **perfect cadence** (bar 12).

B   **(Theme 2)** Contrast: 'minor' sound. End of bar 12 – bar 16.
One 4-bar phrase. Phrase begins at a higher **pitch** and with a **minor** sound created by the chords of A minor and D minor, ending with an **imperfect cadence** (bar 16).

A1   **(Theme 1, first varied repeat)** Ionian mode – 'major' sound. Bar 17 – bar 21.
One 4-bar phrase. Phrase **repeats** material from Theme 1 with some **variation**, including a reversal of the notes in the opening **anacrusis**, and an extension in the length of the **perfect cadence** at the end of the phrase (bars 20–21).

C   **(Theme 3)** Contrast: Aeolian mode – 'minor' sound. Bar 22 – bar 29.
Two 4-bar phrases. First phrase establishes contrasting **minor** sound through the use of the *Aeolian* **mode** and the **chords** of A minor and E minor (**tonic** and **dominant** chords in the Aeolian mode). Second phrase introduces a new **semiquaver** (sixteenth note) **rhythm** in bars 27 and 29, ending with an **imperfect cadence** at bar 29.

A2   **(Theme 1, second varied repeat)** Ionian mode – 'major' sound. End of bar 29 – bar 38.
Two 4-bar phrases, both of which **repeat** much of the material of Theme 1 with some **variation**, including the addition of an extra bar in **2/4 time** (bar 38) to extend the length of the **perfect cadence** at the end of the second phrase.

D   **(Piano instrumental)** Aeolian mode – 'minor' sound. Bar 39 – bar 46.
Two 4-bar phrases. The instrumental section consists of a **repeat** of Theme 3, where the piano plays both **melody** and **accompaniment**.

A3   **Coda (third varied repeat of Theme 1)** Ionian mode – 'major' sound. End of bar 46 – bar 63.
Two phrases of irregular length. The **Coda** is based on a **varied repeat** of Theme 1, where the **metre** is changed to **3/4 time** and **augmentation** used on some of the notes, creating the feeling that the music is slowing down for a more expressive conclusion.

Adding Lyrics

I mentioned at the start of this workshop that I would not be writing lyrics to 'Scots Song' but that you should do so for your own song (*and* mine, if you fancy a little extra practice).

Your lyrics will have to fit with the *mood* and *style* of the song as well as its **rhythms** and phrase structure, and you should consider the use of both **melismatic** and **syllabic** vocal writing. Just try to let the atmosphere of the melody conjure up ideas and images in your mind which you can convert into words.

If at a later stage you decide to compose another Scots song or ballad based on an existing text such as a poem (or perhaps lyrics you have written yourself), you can still, of course, follow the various composing steps used in this workshop, ensuring that your **themes** (or **verses** and **choruses**) fit the **rhythm** of your chosen words.

Extension Ideas

Arranging 'Scots Song' for a larger instrumental group

With the music and lyrics of your song written, you could go on to expand the piece by adding more instruments, perhaps arranging it for a **folk group** or even a small choir (with or without the piano accompaniment). This could become a recording project undertaken as part of your *Sound Engineering and Production* work (if you have chosen this option as part of *Performing with Technology*).

Developing 'Scots Song' using a MIDI sequencer

Alternatively, you might choose to **arrange** your song using a computer and a MIDI sequencing programme. (For guidelines on MIDI sequencing techniques see the arranging workshop on page 41.)

That is how I went on to arrange 'Scots Song'. Using the sequencer I kept the original piano accompaniment in the **mix** but applied several different instrument sounds (patches) to play the **melody,** and then went on to add **chords**, **arpeggios** and a new **bass** part. I also composed a drum track which added extra depth to the music.

The chart (or **track sheet**) on the following page shows details of each track in my MIDI sequencing arrangement of 'Scots Song'. Note the sound patches used for the **melody, chord**, **arpeggio** and **bass** parts, and how some of these only play at certain sections in the arrangement; this kind of variety helps to create an interesting **mix**. Another very important aspect of the **mix** is the *volume level* of each patch; without these different volumes the piece would not be balanced since certain sounds which are naturally louder or have a more prominent *timbre* would overwhelm the others.

TRACK	PATCH (sound)	VOLUME (max = 127)	MUSIC PLAYED
1	Ocarina	90	**Melody** (except at *Instrumental* section)
2	Whistle	80	**Melody** (played two octaves higher than original vocal pitch)
3	Pad 4 choir	80	**Melody**
4	Piccolo	65	**Melody** (at *Instrumental* section only)
5	Oboe	28	**Melody** (at *Instrumental* section only)
6	Accordion	60	**Melody** at *Coda* section and **arpeggios** in bars 22–30
7	Acoustic grand piano	100	Original **piano accompaniment**
8	Synth strings 1	40	**Sustained Chords** (based on piano accompaniment)
9	Hammond organ	40	**Sustained Chords** in bars 13–19 and bars 48–65
10	Choir Aahs	45	**Sustained Chords** in bars 13–31 and bars 39–65
11	Orchestral harp	50	**Arpeggios** (at *Instrumental* section only) based on piano accompaniment
12	Tubular bells	80	**Single notes** mainly on the first beat of each bar in the *Coda* section
13	Electric bass guitar (finger)	65	**Bass part** derived from chords used in piano accompaniment
14	Drums	70	**Basic steady beat** with some links/drum fills

CD Track 57. You can hear my full arrangement of 'Scots Song', produced entirely using the MIDI sequencer, on CD track 57. As an extra guide, the music of the first eight bars of this arrangement is given below.

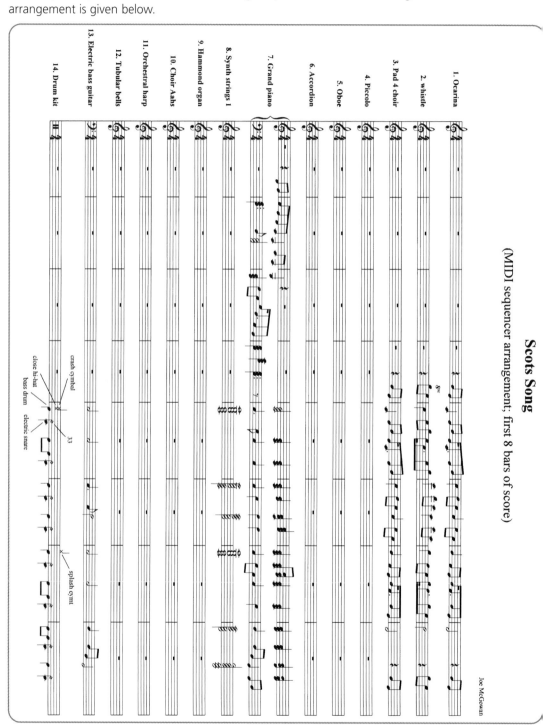

Programme Note	**'Scots Song'**	**by Joe McGowan**

Stimulus

My enjoyment of traditional Scottish vocal music inspired me to compose a Scots song with piano accompaniment in which I could incorporate some of the new musical techniques and concepts I have encountered in Higher Music. I particularly like the emotive, sometimes haunting melodies created by the modes which are often used in Scottish music, and this had a strong influence on the melody of 'Scots Song'.

Resources

Manuscript paper, piano, MIDI keyboard and sequencer

Significant Decisions

Although based on a traditional style, I decided to make the structure of my Scots song a little different by developing it from three main themes and creating a more through-composed framework rather than using the common verse-chorus-verse format. The first theme is in the 'major-sounding' Ionian mode, whereas the second incorporates minor chords which create a contrasting darker sound, and the third theme is in the Aeolian mode (which also has a minor sound).

Use of technology

Using the MIDI sequencer I was able to hear and check each step of composition in 'Scots Song'. When I had completed the piece I then arranged it on the sequencer using a much larger number of instruments/sounds (14 in total) experimenting with various sound patch combinations and making extensive use of the editing functions. I then saved my arrangement as a MIDI file which I burned onto CD before finally printing out the score.

Use of improvisation

I improvised in various modes and pentatonic scales to generate the ideas and phrases which eventually became the melodic material for this piece.

Audio Recording Arrangements

I made a live recording of 'Scots Song' in which a fellow student sang the melody (the lyrics of which I wrote myself) and my teacher played the piano accompaniment. I later mixed this recording in the studio and added it to my Sound Engineering and Production folio.

Process

I began by improvising in several modes and pentatonic scales (and using various chord notes) to get the first melodic ideas which became Theme 1. I repeated this process for the other two main themes in which I also used variation, modulation and a metre change from 4/4 to 3/4 at the Coda. After completing the melody I wrote the piano accompaniment (including a 4-bar introduction) based upon chords I had already worked out for each bar as I was writing the melody.

Workshop 4: Composing 'Jazzin' Around'

We are now going to compose a piece of jazz music based on a rhythmic **ostinato** over which a melody will be **improvised**. Owing to the style and length of this work the music notation for the entire piece is not shown at the end, but musical examples and CD excerpts of the important structural landmarks are provided at each main step of composition.

This workshop can be undertaken as a MIDI sequencing exercise, since a MIDI sequencer was used to compose the piece of music featured, and references are made to the processes involved in composing with this kind of software. However, it is not essential to use a MIDI sequencer, and the workshop can be tackled by those who prefer to write for 'live' instruments.

Before we begin, let's take a look at how jazz music gets its 'jazzy' sound.

Jazz chords

The characteristic sound of jazz music is produced mainly from the way in which extra notes are added to basic chords (these are called chord *extensions*), and certain chord notes are 'sharpened' or 'flattened' to create different sounds (or harmonies). For example, the basic **triad** of G major is, like all other *primary* chords, made up of the *first*, *third* and *fifth* notes of its scale (G, B, D). If we add the note E to the G chord we now have a four-note chord consisting of G, B, D and E. Because E is the *sixth* note in the G major scale, the new chord is called **G6** or **G added 6th**. It's that straightforward!

Since, in any key, the first, third and fifth notes of a scale form a basic **chord**, that leaves us with the second, fourth, sixth and seventh notes to play around with.

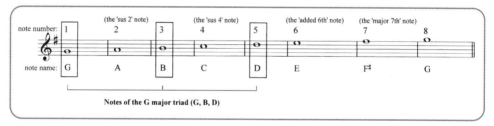

Common chord extensions
The suspended second (or sus 2) chord

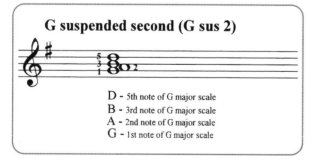

This chord consists of the basic **triad** plus the *second* note of the scale, meaning that the 1st, 2nd, 3rd and 5th notes of the chord's scale are used. The word 'suspended', abbreviated to 'sus', just means that the addition of the second note creates a **suspension** or suspended effect in the music which will normally be **resolved** in the chord which follows. This **resolution** usually involves a **stepwise** move up or down onto a note in the next chord.

The sus 2 chord is not used very often (although it is sometimes seen in modern pop and rock music) as it is normally replaced by the far more common **added 9th chord** (see page 100).

The suspended fourth (or sus 4) chord

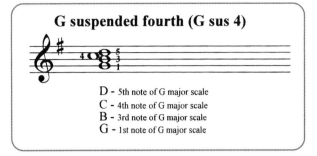

G suspended fourth (G sus 4)

D - 5th note of G major scale
C - 4th note of G major scale
B - 3rd note of G major scale
G - 1st note of G major scale

When a basic **triad** has the fourth note of its scale added to it, the chord becomes a *suspended fourth* or *sus 4*. Behaving in the same way as a sus 2 chord, the sus 4 will normally be 'resolved' in the chord which follows. Try playing a G sus 4 followed by a plain G chord and you will hear the **suspension** and **resolution** effect (notice how this creates *tension* then *relaxation* in the music).

Hints and Tips

In **renaissance**, **baroque** and **classical** music the **suspension** and **resolution** chords would normally be preceded by a **preparation** chord which contains the **suspension** note. In the key of G major, for example, one such chord progression would be: *C major* (the **preparation** chord containing the **suspension** note, **C**), then *G sus 4* (the **suspension** chord containing the **suspension** note, **C**), and finally *G major* (the **resolution** chord where the 4th note, **C**, **resolves** back down to **B**). Play this chord progression (C major – G sus 4 – G major) to hear the effect.

The added 6th (or 6th) chord

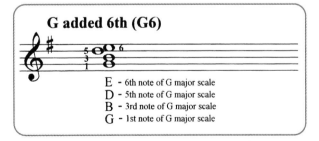

G added 6th (G6)

E - 6th note of G major scale
D - 5th note of G major scale
B - 3rd note of G major scale
G - 1st note of G major scale

The **added 6th chord** is simply the basic **triad** with the 6th note of its scale added, meaning that the 1st, 3rd, 5th and 6th notes of the scale are used.

The augmented chord

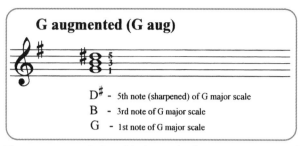

The **augmented chord** is formed when we 'augment' (raise or 'sharpen') the 5th note of a major chord by one **semitone**. The notes in a G augmented chord are therefore G, B, and D♯. Notice that all the notes in an augmented chord are a **major third interval** apart.

7th chords

Here is where some interesting things happen!

Several types of 7th chord are commonly used – not just in jazz but in other types of music as well. These are the **major 7th**, the **dominant 7th**, the **minor 7th,** and the **diminished 7th**.

The major 7th chord

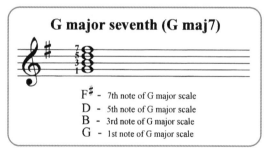

When the seventh note of a major scale is added to its **tonic** chord (chord **I**) we get the major 7th chord. That is because the **interval** between the first and seventh notes of the scale is a major 7th.

The dominant 7th chord

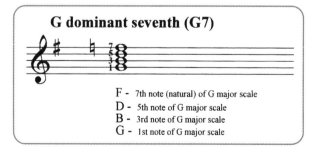

When the 'seventh' note of the major 7th chord is lowered (flattened) by one **semitone** we get a **dominant 7th chord**. In the key of G major this means that the F♯ (F sharp) in the G major 7th chord is lowered to F♮ (F natural). This chord is called the dominant 7th because it is formed from the **dominant** chord of a key, not the **tonic**. For example, G major is the **dominant** chord (V) in the key of C major, and in this key the seventh note is F♮.

Hints and Tips

Students sometimes get the major 7th and dominant 7th chords confused with each other. An easy way to remember the difference is to understand that the 'major 7th' refers to the **interval** (a major 7th) between the first and seventh notes of the chord. A G major 7th chord is therefore a G chord which includes the major 7th interval (G – F♯), whereas in G dominant 7th (G7) this interval is a minor 7th (G – F♮). Putting it another way, the word 'major' in a G major 7th chord refers to the *major* 7th interval, not to the fact that the chord itself is major. (Think of G major 7th therefore as a *G chord* with a major 7th, not as *G major* with a 7th.)

The minor 7th chord

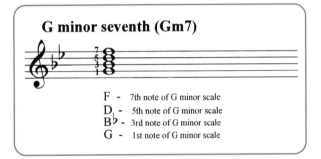

G minor seventh (Gm7)

F – 7th note of G minor scale
D – 5th note of G minor scale
B♭ – 3rd note of G minor scale
G – 1st note of G minor scale

The minor seventh chord is formed when we take a **minor triad** and to it add the seventh note of its scale.

The diminished 7th chord

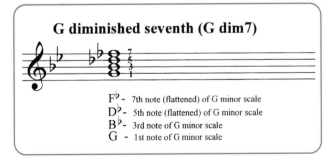

G diminished seventh (G dim7)

F♭ – 7th note (flattened) of G minor scale
D♭ – 5th note (flattened) of G minor scale
B♭ – 3rd note of G minor scale
G – 1st note of G minor scale

A **diminished 7th chord** is formed when we lower both the 5th and 7th notes of a minor 7th chord by one **semitone**. In the chord of G diminished seventh, therefore, the notes are G, B♭, **D♭** and **F♭**. (Notice that all the notes in a diminished seventh chord are a **minor third interval** apart.)

Hints and Tips

These four versions of the seventh chord might seem a little complex at first, but playing them a few times on a keyboard will help you to hear and *see* what is happening in each chord. It might also help to imagine these chords stacked up in a kind of *tower* with the major 7th chord at the top (since the distance between its notes – the **intervals** – is the *largest*) and the diminished 7th at the bottom (because the distance between its notes is the *smallest*).

Major 7th
Dominant 7th
Minor 7th
Diminished 7th

↕

Largest distance between notes

Smallest distance between notes (all *minor 3rd* **intervals**)

Other extension chords: the added 9th, 11th and 13th

As there are eight notes in a one-**octave** scale, any chord which displays a number larger than eight – such as G9, C11, E13 – contains an **interval** larger than an octave. For example, a G9 chord is based on a G major **triad** with the ninth note above the root note (first note [G]) added. The same applies to the added 11th and 13th chords.

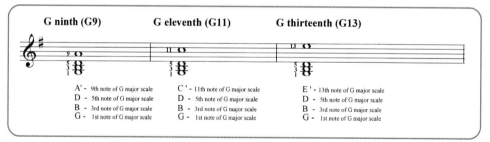

In jazz music we can add just about any note to a basic **chord** to create expressive and sometimes unusual and **discordant** sounds which are used for their individual 'colour'.

There are many types of chords commonly used in jazz music where certain notes are raised or lowered (often by a **semitone**) to produce 'altered' chords such as the *flattened fifth*, *augmented fifth* and *flattened ninth*.

Any note in a chord can be sharpened or flattened, and more than one 'extra' note (or extension) can be added to a basic **triad**, so various combinations are also possible. For example:

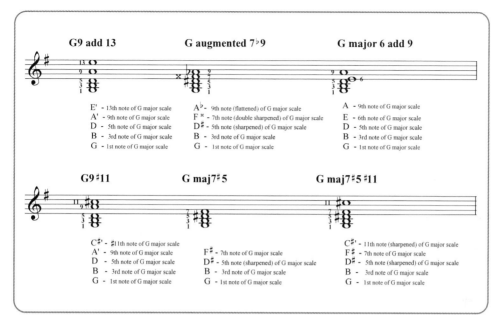

Although all of the above extension chords contain either four or five different notes, sometimes the 3rd or (more often) the 5th note of the basic triad is left out of the chord. This is done particularly with the 5th note because a chord can still retain its characteristic sound without it, and also because omitting it can make extension chords easier to play on an instrument such as the guitar.

For Practice

Have some fun experimenting with the chords described above, and try making up your own by adding sharps, flats and extra notes to basic chords – remember that you can also remove notes from a chord (the 5th note for instance) and use chord **inversions**. If possible, try to name the chords you play (for example, G7, G add 9), but this isn't necessary to come up with some really cool sounds!

Step 1: The plan

If you have worked through the previous two composing workshops you will be familiar with the planning processes involved, so here, to begin, is the plan for my jazz piece:

◆ Two main sections, joined together by a short **link** passage: first section (A) in a **major key**, second section (B) will be faster and in a new key

◆ Key of section A: G major. Section B will **modulate** to another key or keys (perhaps the **dominant** or **relative minor** key); a **modulation** will take place in the **link** passage

◆ Rhythmic **ostinato** consisting of various instruments (including bass guitar and drums) over which two **solo** instruments, piano and vibraphone, will play an **improvisatory** melody based on several melodic ideas or fragments

◆ May use **major**, **minor** and **pentatonic** scales

◆ Use **chromaticism**, **syncopation**, **sequence**, **imitation**, **transposition** and **variation**

◆ Give bass guitar a **melodic** role in B section

Structure plan

Owing to the free, improvised style of this piece the structure plan is very simple. Any complexity in the music will come from the **improvisation** of the two **solo** instruments.

A Section (moderate tempo) Key: G major	Link passage Modulation into the key of the B section	B Section (faster) New key
Melody: Piano begins an **improvisation** based on one of several melodic ideas, followed by entry of vibraphone (perhaps with a new melodic idea). This begins the 'conversation' (often with **Question** and **Answer** phrases) between these two **solo** instruments which is **developed** throughout the piece. **Accompaniment:** **Rhythmic ostinato** played by bass guitar, drums and other instruments playing **chords. Sequence** will be used in this rhythm section.	Short **link** to **modulate** into the new **key** and faster **tempo** of the B section, perhaps based on a **chromatic** passage.	**Melody:** Livelier music with the two **solo** instruments **improvising** around new melodic ideas. **Accompaniment:** **Rhythmic ostinato** altered in some way; also **transposed** into the new **key** and played faster, with bass guitar having a more **melodic** role. May **modulate** into more than one new key in this section.

Hints and Tips

Before making a plan for your own piece, listen to a variety of jazz music to give yourself some ideas and inspiration, paying careful attention to features such as **rhythm**, **style**, **improvisation** and the way musical instruments are used.

Step 2: Composing the ostinato rhythm

The rhythm section of this piece will be the foundation (the 'backing') on which the entire composition is built.

Having listened to many recordings of different kinds of jazz music for inspiration, I was particularly attracted to the catchy **bossa nova**, a **Latin-American** jazz style with this characteristic rhythm:

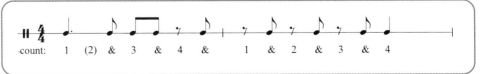

I immediately began experimenting with this **rhythm** on the MIDI keyboard and sequencer using jazz extension chords in the key of G major, such as added 6ths, 7ths, 9ths and so on, and soon arrived at an 8-bar chord progression which sounded good. These eight bars of music will be **repeated**, sometimes using **harmonic sequence** and **modulation**, all through my jazz piece, to form the **ostinato** rhythm.

CD Track 58. Below is the music of this 8-bar chord progression, based on the *bossa nova* rhythm, which you can hear on CD track 58. The chord progression is played by a combination of two different sounds (or *patches*) playing in **unison**; these are *rock organ* and *acoustic guitar (nylon)* from the MIDI sound set.

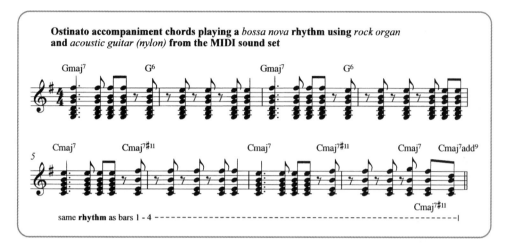

Ostinato accompaniment chords playing a *bossa nova* **rhythm using** *rock organ* and *acoustic guitar (nylon)* **from the MIDI sound set**

same **rhythm** as bars 1 - 4

For Practice

Start off your own piece now by working out a jazz chord progression which can be **repeated** as an **ostinato** rhythm section – or, if you prefer not to have an **ostinato**, you might instead choose to experiment with lots of different jazz chords and build up a fairly long and constantly changing chord progression to improvise over.

To add some depth to my **ostinato** rhythm, I added another part using the same **chords** but with different note values (semibreves or whole notes). In this part only one **sustained** chord was used for each bar using a combination of *Pad 2 (warm)* and *Synth voice* sounds from the MIDI sound set.

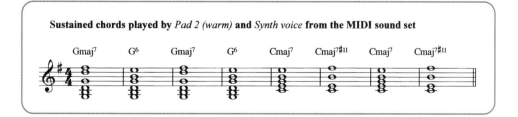

Sustained chords played by *Pad 2 (warm)* and *Synth voice* **from the MIDI sound set**

Sustained chords are a very effective type of accompaniment to include in many kinds of musical composition, since they help to keep the music flowing whilst firmly establishing the harmony.

For Practice

If you wish, try adding **sustained chords** to your accompaniment now. Remember that these chords should *enhance* rather than *conflict* with the main accompaniment rhythm, so choose an instrument/sound patch (such as *strings*) which is not only capable of sustaining long notes but will also blend well with the other parts.

With the **chords** and **rhythm** of my **ostinato** accompaniment taken care of, the next task involves adding bass guitar and drum parts. These should not 'drown out' the bossa nova rhythm, so they mustn't be too complicated, but having them merely imitate the accompaniment rhythm might make them sound dull and unadventurous, so we need to add some rhythmic **variation** – without overdoing it.

The bass guitar part

For the bass guitar part of my rhythm section I started off by experimenting with **chord notes** from the 8-bar **ostinato** progression, and from this an idea for a simple **syncopated** melody came to me (which didn't interfere with the bossa nova rhythm). I decided to make this the first of the main melodic ideas outlined in my plan for the piece.

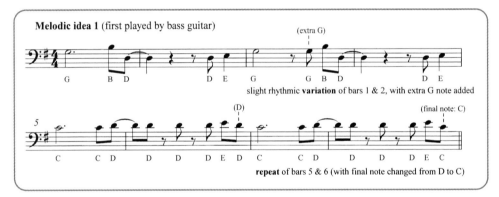

This melodic idea will be **repeated** throughout the A section by the bass guitar (as an **ostinato**) and **developed** by the two **solo** instruments.

 CD Track 59. Listen to the bass guitar playing melodic idea 1 over the 8-bar rhythmic **ostinato** figure (which now includes the sustained chords) on CD track 59. You will hear that I have **mixed** the track so that the bass guitar is louder than the accompaniment chords.

For Practice

Now compose a bass part for your accompaniment. This might involve adding only single notes at the start of each bar (determined by the accompaniment chords) or, as in my piece, a **syncopated** melodic idea. If you choose to write a melodic idea, be careful that it doesn't conflict with the music you have already written.

The drum and percussion part

Using a MIDI sequencer to compose this piece meant that lots of drum and percussion sounds were available to me (in fact I had great fun experimenting with combining the various sounds!).

A drum part often has several different components (*bass drum*, *snare*, *tom-tom*, *hi-hat* and so on), so unless you are an experienced drummer a good way to compose this part will be to build it up gradually by adding one sound at a time. You might, for instance, 'hear' instinctively where the hi-hat or a **drum fill** would sound good, or begin by laying down a steady **bass drum** beat and then try out other percussion sounds on top of this. That is exactly how I composed my own drum/percussion part, beginning with *acoustic bass drum* and *close hi-hat*, then adding *cabasa*, *tambourine* and *33* (a percussive sound effect) from the MIDI drum kit sounds, until I was satisfied that I had a good drum track to fit with my **ostinato** accompaniment.

CD Track 60. Below are the four bars of music for my drum/percussion part which will be **repeated** all through section A of the piece – you can listen to them on CD track 60. Don't be daunted by how complex the music *looks*; some of the notes have cross or diamond-shaped note heads just so that it is easier to identify individual instruments in the part – and remember, this part was simply 'stitched' together by adding one sound at a time.

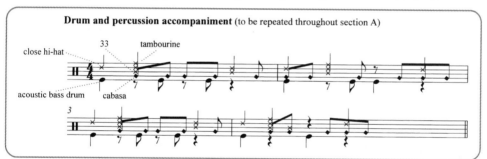

Drum and percussion accompaniment (to be repeated throughout section A)

On the following page you can see the eight bars of music (showing the four individual parts or tracks) which will be **repeated** to form the **ostinato** accompaniment for the whole of section A of my piece.

CD Track 61. I extended this 8-bar **ostinato** to a total of thirty-eight bars, making my A section, with a **tempo** of ♩ = 95, last for one minute and thirty-three seconds. I made just one or two alterations to the **ostinato** along the way, changing the **chords** to C major (first inversion) and F major in bars 13–17 and 29–33, and altering the occasional note in the bass part, but otherwise the **ostinato** remains constant for the whole A section. Listen to it on CD track 61 and then, for practice (or just fun), try **improvising** over it with your choice of instrument – remember that the key is G major. Doing this will help when you come to work on the improvised **solos** for your own piece. Enjoy!

For Practice

Complete your accompaniment by adding a drum and percussion part now. If you are using a MIDI sequencer you will enjoy experimenting with the many different drum and percussion sounds there are to choose from. Take your time to work on the part, trying out various sound combinations as you gradually build it up.

When you have done this you can **repeat** your **ostinato** figure (if you are using one) as many times as you like to form the 'backing' for your improvised **solo** part(s). You should consider using **sequence** and **variation** in the **ostinato** accompaniment, but be careful not to overdo it as the purpose of the ostinato in this case is to provide a repetitive and unobtrusive background of sound over which other music will be played.

Hints *and* Tips

◆ Repeating whole sections of music is an easy task with a MIDI sequencer because, rather like using a word processor, all you have to do is *copy* the section to be repeated and *paste* it wherever you want it to occur in the piece. Techniques such as **harmonic sequence** are also easily undertaken since again you can *copy* a section of music, *paste* it wherever you want it to **repeat**, select *edit – transpose* and then simply choose by what **interval** you want to raise or lower its **pitch**.

◆ Using the *Loop* function on the MIDI sequencer, you can play back a part (or several parts) in a continuously repeating cycle, which enables you to try out new sounds or melodic ideas on top of the repeating music.

◆ When using a sequencer you are not restricted as to an instrument's **range** or the number of notes it can play simultaneously, since **pitches** and note combinations which are well beyond the scope of a real instrument can be created on the sequencer. We can, for example, have a *flute* sound playing **chords**, or producing notes an **octave** or more above or below the normal **range** of that instrument.

Step 3: The improvised solo parts

This step involves working out two separate improvised **solo** parts (for piano and vibraphone in my case) to play over the **ostinato** accompaniment.

I chose the vibraphone (a **pitched percussion** instrument similar to a glockenspiel, but with electrically powered resonating tubes) for its clarity and because its sound fits well with the piano – yet is sufficiently different to create **contrast** – but also because it is used in many kinds of jazz music.

I had two options for how I went about developing these **solo** improvisations: I could either record some 'live' spontaneous improvisations using the MIDI keyboard and sequencer, or compose music in an improvisatory style and record it note-for-note on the sequencer. Although a bit more time-consuming, I went for the second option as I wanted the piano and vibraphone parts to sound really closely integrated with each other and I felt this would be more difficult to achieve with 'live' improvisation.

When two instruments are **improvising** at the same time it demands a certain amount of skill on the part of the player/composer to combine the parts in such a way that they don't conflict with each other, or sound as though they are playing completely unrelated improvisations – which would upset the balance of the music. You should try to make such an improvisation sound as though the two instruments are having a *conversation* – as opposed to an argument over who should be playing at that point!

One good way of handling this is to think of the improvised parts as a *single* improvisation which you have to split into two parts: one part for each instrument. Here are some helpful points to keep in mind when building up an **improvisation** with two (or more) instruments:

- Have one instrument play a **Question** phrase which is then **Answered** by the other instrument.
- As one instrument plays a passage, have the other **harmonise** it with notes which are a *third*, a *sixth* or an *octave* higher or lower.
- Instruments can play passages in **unison**.
- Have the instruments play sections using **canon** (staggered entries of the same music).
- One instrument can **repeat** a passage of music played earlier by another instrument.
- Instruments can **imitate** each other, or parts of the **accompaniment**.
- Vary between instruments playing together and separately.

Other possible techniques for a jazz improvisation

- **Syncopation**
- Choose **chord notes** from the **accompaniment** part
- Choose notes used in *extension chords* such as the added 6th, 9th, 11th and 13th
- **Chromaticism**
- **Staccato/legato** passages
- Experiment with a wide variety of different **rhythms**
- Contrasting **dynamics**

I decided to begin the **solo improvisation** with the piano playing a new melodic idea which would fit the moderate speed and laid-back style of the **ostinato** accompaniment. Taking into account the **syncopated** character of the first main melodic idea played by bass guitar, I opted to use this feature in the piano **improvisation** whilst still creating an entirely new **melody** that would stand out from the other parts.

CD Track 62. You can hear what I came up with for the opening part of the piano **improvisation** (playing over the **ostinato** accompaniment) on CD track 62, the music of which (*melodic idea 2*) is written on the following page. Melodic idea 1 (bass guitar) and melodic idea 2 (piano), played simultaneously at the start of my piece, will form the basic material which is **developed** by the piano and vibraphone **solo** parts throughout the A section.

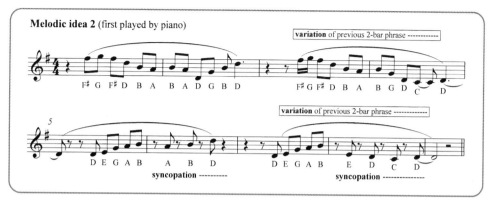

Melodic idea 2 (first played by piano)

variation of previous 2-bar phrase -----------

F# G F# D B A   B A D G B D

F# G F# D B A   B G D C D

variation of previous 2-bar phrase -------------

D E G A B   A   B   D

D E G A B   E   D C   D

syncopation ----------

syncopation ---------------

CD Track 63. Due to space limitations, the full musical score for the A section cannot be shown here, but below is a structure chart detailing how I went on to **develop** the entire A section from the two melodic ideas (bass guitar and piano) described above. Look carefully at the important musical events and where they occur in the music, and particularly the ways in which I **develop** my two central melodic ideas. You can follow the chart while you listen to my finished A section on CD track 63; do this several times until you become familiar with the music and its structure. To help you locate specific 'landmarks' the precise time at which each important event occurs is shown in *brackets* beside the bar numbers.

A SECTION			
Bar no. *(time)*:	**Bar 1 *(00.01)***	**Bar 9 *(00.20)***	**Bar 13 *(00.31)***
Piano:	Melodic idea 2	silent	Plays a **variation** of the second phrase of **Melodic idea 2**, including a 'flourish' of **semiquavers** (sixteenth notes) in bar 16 *(00.38)*
Vibraphone:	silent	Plays a **variation** of **Melodic idea 1** an **octave** higher than bass guitar	Continues playing a **variation** of **Melodic idea 1** which overlaps with the piano to create **counterpoint**
Bass guitar:	Melodic idea 1		
Ostinato accompaniment chords:	**G major 7** and **G6;** **C major 7** and **C major 7#11**		**C major** (first inversion) and **F major**

Bar no. *(time):*	Bar 17 *(00.40)*	Bar 25 *(01.01)*	Bar 29 *(01.11)*
Piano:	Free improvisation where both instruments **imitate** each other's melodic fragments (one **octave** apart), and piano plays another flourish of semiquavers (bar 24, *00.58*)	Both instruments play a **variation** of **Melodic idea 1** in **unison octaves** (they play the same music one octave apart)	Plays a **variation** of fragments used in **Melodic idea 1**
Vibraphone:			Plays a highly **syncopated variation** of **Melodic idea 1** and **imitates** the **semiquaver flourish** (bar 31, *01.17*) first played by piano in bar 16
Bass guitar:	Melodic idea 1 (cont.)		
Ostinato accompaniment chords:	**G major 7** and **G6**; **C major 7** and **C major 7♯11**		**C major** (first inversion) and **F major**

Bar no. *(time):*	Bar 33 *(01.21)*	Bar 38 *(01.33)*
Piano:	**Repeats** a fragment from **Melodic idea 2**, followed by a single bar of **descending** notes (bar 36, *01.28*) which closes the A section melody	silent
Vibraphone:	**Repeats** the first 3 bars of **Theme 1** (varied), followed by a single bar of **descending syncopated** notes (bar 36, *01.28*) which closes the A section melody	silent
Bass guitar:	Melodic idea 1 (cont.)	silent
Ostinato accompaniment chords:	**G major 7** and **G6**	silent (only drums will play here)

For Practice

Using my A section as a source of reference (and hopefully inspiration!), create an **improvisation** for either one or two instruments to play over the accompaniment in your own piece now. Remember that you can approach this the way I did by composing melodic ideas and then **developing** them (or **improvising** around them), or, you might instead prefer to record some spontaneous 'live' improvisations and keep the best ones for your final **mix**. If you decide to compose parts of your **improvisation**, try to make the music sound relaxed and spontaneous – nice and *cool*. Take your time, enjoy the process of making the music, and you are sure to produce something good.

Step 4: The B section

Rather than compose the **link** passage now, I am going straight on to the B section of my piece as I will know better how to link the two contrasting A and B sections once I can listen to them side-by-side.

In my structure plan I decided that the B section was going to be in a different **key** and faster **tempo** than the A section in order to create **contrast** and **develop** the piece, but I didn't want the new section to sound disjointed from the first, so I kept the *bossa nova* accompaniment rhythm going to preserve a sense of **unity**.

After some experimentation with different keys, I liked the sound produced when the **pitch** of the **ostinato** chords was **transposed** up a minor third **interval** into the key of B minor (this was an easy task with the MIDI sequencer since all I had to do was *copy* the **chords** from the **ostinato** part in section A, *paste* them, then choose *edit – transpose* to change their key).

The new **ostinato** sounded good in the minor key, but it was still a bit too similar to that of the A section, and I knew I would need to change something if I was to prevent the music from sounding dull and repetitive.

The first thing I did was alter the sound patch combination of *rock organ* and *acoustic guitar (nylon)*, which was used for the **chords** in section A, to *rock organ* and *vibraphone*. I then tried inserting some **chromatic chords**, which instantly gave me the idea that I should perhaps change the chord progression *completely*, whilst still keeping the *bossa nova* rhythm intact. The result (shown below) was an **ostinato** based on a B minor 7th chord and a **chromatic** chord of B♭ minor 7th.

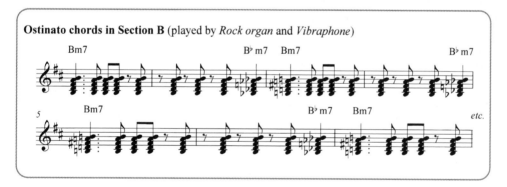

Ostinato chords in Section B (played by *Rock organ* and *Vibraphone*)

The next task involved increasing the **tempo** from ♩ = 95 to a livelier ♩ = 165, which was again done quickly thanks to the sequencer. I really liked the sound of the *bossa nova* rhythm in the new **key** and livelier **tempo**, but still felt that the music needed 'something' else. The obvious places to try something new now were the bass and drum/percussion parts, so again I set about experimenting with new ideas for these tracks.

It was my intention from the planning stage to give the bass guitar a more prominent **melodic** role in the B section anyway, so here was the perfect time to introduce the third main melodic idea into my piece:

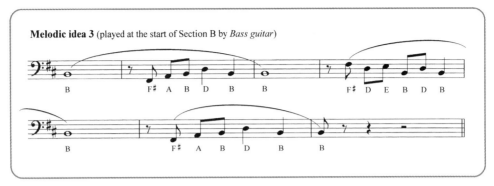

Melodic idea 3 (played at the start of Section B by *Bass guitar*)

Next, I turned my attention to the drums, trying out various drum and percussion sounds until I had composed a new figure for this part which could be **repeated** as an **ostinato**. The figure, shown below, is just two bars long this time.

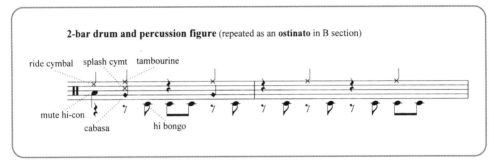

2-bar drum and percussion figure (repeated as an **ostinato** in B section)

CD Track 64. You can hear these parts combined now in my new **ostinato** accompaniment for the B section on CD track 64, the first 7 bars of which are shown on the following page. I have temporarily removed the **sustained chords** from the accompaniment at this stage; these chords will return (played by *Strings 1*) a few bars later, after the entry of the first **solo** part.

First 7 bars of B section

As in section A, I will add **variations** to this **ostinato** accompaniment as I **develop** the new section (in my plan I noted the possibility of changing key more than once), but now I have the main foundation upon which I can build my **solo** parts.

For Practice

If you feel you would like to inject a sudden element of **contrast** into your own piece (perhaps by changing **key** and/or **tempo** as I have), carefully consider the steps described above before experimenting with new **melodic** and **harmonic** ideas that you might include.

Step 5: The improvised solos for section B

The new **key** and **tempo** of the B section created all kinds of possibilities for the two **solo** improvisation parts, so, to begin, I set the sequencer to play the **ostinato** accompaniment in a *loop* and began to **improvise** on the MIDI keyboard in the key of B minor to generate some ideas. I tried both the **harmonic** and **melodic** versions of the B minor scale (see glossary, page 121), but preferred the sound of the B **pentatonic minor** scale and, using this, composed the fourth melodic idea. This idea, which will be played first by piano, consists of four 'mini' phrases of varying length, each separated by **rests** which help to create the feeling of a spontaneous improvisation.

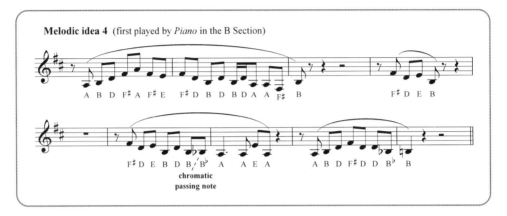

After I had recorded this new melodic idea over the **ostinato** accompaniment I was immediately struck by the thought that it would sound more effective if the accompaniment 'dropped out' (stopped playing) for the first two bars of the new melody (meaning that the piano would be the only instrument playing at this point), after which it would 'drop in' (resume playing) again.

CD Track 65. You can hear the new melodic idea, and the effect created when the **accompaniment** 'drops out' for the first two bars of this music, on CD track 65. The track begins at bar 1 of the B section *(00.01)*, and the piano enters at bar 7 *(00.09)*. You will also hear the entry of the **sustained chords** in bar 9 *(00.12)* played by *Strings 1* from the sound set.

I really liked the sound of the accompaniment dropping out and in like this, and decided to **repeat** the effect later when the vibraphone entered. But before that I wanted to **develop** the piano **solo** a little more, and so began playing around with some new ideas as well as those I had already written to see what I could produce.

The resulting music for the piano, from bar 15 *(00.22)* to bar 29 *(00.42)*, involves a **pedal** of B notes (spanning three **octaves** in **pitch**) based on the **rhythm** of the accompaniment, among which fragments of melodic idea 4 (played an **octave** higher this time) appear. The bass guitar also **imitates** the piano in some bars of this section.

The rising **pitch** of the piano's **pedal** notes really increased the drama, creating the feeling that something was about to happen in the music. It seemed like the ideal time, therefore, to **modulate** into another **key**.

The 'obvious' modulations were *B major*, *E minor* (the **subdominant** key, **IV**), *F♯ major* (the **dominant** key, **V**) and *G major* (the **relative major** key – already used for section A). However, influenced by the use of **chromatic** chords in the **ostinato** accompaniment, I decided to use **chromaticism** again, but this time as a means of **modulating** into the new key (**chromaticism** is now being employed as a kind of 'theme' in the B section).

A straightforward rise in **pitch** of one **tone** (a major second **interval**) took me into the key of C♯ minor, and although this isn't one of the more obvious keys, the **chromatic** progression from B minor – C minor – C♯ minor produced the effect I wanted. All I had to do then to make the **modulation** was use the chord progression B minor – C minor – C♯ minor in the **ostinato** accompaniment, and the notes B – C – C♯ in the piano **solo**. This would leave the way open for the vibraphone to enter in the new key, C♯ minor, at bar 29 (*00.41*).

CD Track 66. You can hear the music just described on CD track 66. Listen carefully for the piano's **pedal** notes, the **repeat** of fragments from melodic idea 4 played an **octave** higher, and the key **modulation** near the end of the excerpt. The track starts at bar 15 (*00.22*) and ends at bar 29 (*00.42*), the point at which the vibraphone will enter with music played in the new key, C♯ minor.

The rise in **pitch** produced by the **key** change seemed to inject a new level of energy into the piece, which I felt would require some even livelier music from the two **solo** parts now. One of the ways I decided to approach this was to have a section where the piano and vibraphone parts had an animated little 'conversation' with each other, sharing a passage of music using **imitation**.

This passage begins with the entry of the vibraphone at bar 29 (*00.42*) – its first appearance in section B – playing the first two bars of melodic idea 4 in the new key of C♯ minor. At bar 32 (*00.46*) it then plays the first of two short phrases which are **imitated** by the piano before the two instruments play a phrase in **unison** at bar 37 (*00.54*). After this, from bar 39 (*00.56*) – bar 43 (*01.02*), both instruments play a **pedal** of (mostly) C♯ notes in **unison octaves**. Throughout this entire section the bass guitar also plays a **pedal** based on the harmony of the **ostinato** rhythm section.

Next, I decided to **repeat** the **imitation** texture again, starting at bar 43 (*01.02*), but now the phrase used for the 'conversation' between piano and vibraphone will be the fifth and final melodic idea (shown below). The new melodic idea is based on just a short 2-bar phrase, but the imitative conversation between the two **solo** instruments will extend and **develop** it in the bars which follow. For a little extra **variation**, this time I also swapped the imitation order around and had the piano play the phrases which are then **imitated** by the vibraphone.

CD Track 67. You can hear the section of music described above (which is a continuation of the previous section heard on track 66) on CD track 67. The music starts with the vibraphone playing the first two bars of melodic idea 4 (in C♯ minor), followed by a phrase (at *00.04*) which begins the first imitative 'conversation' between it and the piano. After this (at *00.12*), for four bars you will then hear the **pedal** notes played by both of these **solo** instruments before the piano enters with melodic idea 5 (at *00.20*), beginning the second imitative 'conversation' shared by the piano and vibraphone.

It now felt as though my piece was leading naturally towards its conclusion, so after the piano and vibraphone had completed their second 'conversation' involving melodic idea 5, from bar 53 (*01.17*) I **repeated** the **unison octave** passage which these instruments first played in bars 39 (*00.56*)–43 (*01.02*), after which I would add a **Codetta** (short **Coda**) to round off the music.

My 3-bar **Codetta**, shown below, is based on a short flourish of notes played by piano and vibraphone in **unison** at the **octave**. The notes are derived from the **key chord** of C♯ minor, together with some **passing notes**, and the **rhythm** of the first bar **repeats** that of melodic idea 5, bar 1. Notice that, in this short conclusion to 'Jazzin' Around', only the piano, vibraphone, bass guitar and drum/percussion parts are playing.

CD Track 68. On pages 117–118 there is a structure chart of my completed B section showing where the important musical events occur. Study it carefully, taking note of how I have re-used and **varied** material to **develop** the section from just a few melodic ideas, then listen to the music on CD track 68 a couple of times whilst carefully following the plan, pausing or skipping back if you need to.

B SECTION			
Bar no. *(time):*	**Bar 1** *(00.01)*	**Bar 7** *(00.10)*	**Bar 9** *(00.13)*
Piano:	silent	**melodic idea 4**	**melodic idea 4** continues
Vibraphone:	silent	silent	silent
Bass guitar:	**melodic idea 3**	silent	**melodic idea 3**
Ostinato accompaniment chords:	**B minor 7** and **B♭ minor 7**	silent	**B minor 7** and **B♭ minor 7**, with **A minor 7** and **B♭ minor 7** used in bars 13–15

Bar no. *(time):*	**Bar 15** *(00.22)*	**Bar 26** *(00.39)*	**Bar 29** *(00.42)*
Piano:	Piano plays a **pedal** of B notes (spanning 3 **octaves**) based on the **rhythm** of the **ostinato** chords. Some fragments from **melodic idea 3** are also used.	1-bar modulation (bar 26–27) into new key of C♯ minor using **chromatic** notes (B-C-C♯), followed by a **pedal** of C♯ notes played in **octaves**	silent
Vibraphone:	silent	silent	**melodic idea 4 transposed** into C♯ minor
Bass guitar:	**melodic idea 3**	silent	silent until bar 31 when it plays a **pedal** of C♯ notes based on the **ostinato rhythm**
Ostinato accompaniment chords:	**B minor 7** and **B♭ minor 7**, with **A minor 7** and **B♭ minor 7** used in bars 21–23	**B minor 7** and **C minor 7**	Silent until bar 31 when the new ostinato chords of **C♯ minor 7** and **C minor 7** begin playing

Bar no. *(time):*	Bar 32 *(00.47)*	Bar 39 *(00.57)*	Bar 43 *(01.03)*
Piano: Vibraphone:	**Imitation** phrases between vibraphone and piano	**Pedal** notes shared between piano and vibraphone in **unison octaves**	Piano plays **melodic idea 5**, beginning a passage in which it shares **Question** and **Answer** phrases with the vibraphone
Bass guitar:	resumes **pedal** notes based on the **rhythm** and **harmony** of the **ostinato** chords		silent until end of bar 44 when it plays a 3-note **anacrusis** to create a **link** into bar 45 when it resumes the **pedal** of C♯ notes
Ostinato accompaniment chords:	**C♯ minor 7** and **C minor 7**, with **B minor 7** in bar 35 and **A minor 7** in bar 36	**C♯ minor 7** and **C minor 7**	Silent until bar 45 when **C♯ minor 7** and **C minor 7** resume

Bar no. *(time):*	Bar 48 *(01.11)*	Bar 53 *(01.17)*	Bar 55 *(01.20)*
Piano: Vibraphone:	Passage played in **unison octaves** between the piano and vibraphone (starting at the end of bar 48) which includes fragments of **melodic idea 4**	Piano and vibraphone play a **pedal** of C♯ notes in **unison octaves** using the **ostinato rhythm**	Piano and vibraphone build the drama and move the piece towards its conclusion by raising the **pitch** of the C♯ **pedal** notes and using **octave doublings**
Bass guitar:	**pedal** notes based on the **rhythm** and **harmony** of the **ostinato** chords		
Ostinato accompaniment chords:	**C♯ minor 7** and **C minor 7**, with **B minor 7** in bars 51–53		

Bar no. *(time):*	Bar 59 *(01.26)*
Piano: Vibraphone:	Short 3-bar 'Codetta' in which piano and vibraphone play a flourish of notes based on chord notes of C♯ minor and the opening rhythm of melodic idea 5
Bass guitar:	3-bar passage of new music to **harmonise** with the piano and vibraphone
Ostinato accompaniment chords:	silent

Step 6: The middle Link passage

Now for the last and (hopefully) easiest task: composing the short **link** passage which will join the A and B sections together.

The most important thing about this small passage of music is that it must link the two main sections in such a way that the effect sounds quite natural, as opposed to creating an obvious 'stitch' in the middle of the piece.

My B section is a good deal faster than the A section, so I could perhaps 'leap' rather dramatically from the end of the A section into the new **key** and **tempo** of the B section (sometimes this technique can be very effective). In this case the **link** might just consist of a passage where the **ostinato** accompaniment plays on its own at the end of section A for a bar or two before launching suddenly into the B section. Alternatively, I could build up the speed more gradually using an **accelerando**.

After trying out both options I felt that the **accelerando** produced the most effective result, especially when combined with a rising passage of **chromatic** notes used to **modulate** from the key of G major (in section A) into B minor (in section B).

You will recall that I used **chromaticism** in a similar way to **modulate** from B minor to C♯ minor half way through the B section, but this time only the bass guitar (playing single notes) is used to carry out the modulation, and the modulation itself takes place over *four* full bars. I chose to give this important part to the bass guitar since it has the most prominent **melodic** role at the beginning of the B section (playing melodic idea 3), and so this **link** passage made a very nice 'introduction' to its part in section B. I also used **diminution** in the **link** passage as an additional means of speeding up the music into the new **tempo** of section B (see the music notation below).

CD Track 69. You can hear the 4-bar **Link** passage on CD track 69, the music for which is written below. The track begins at the end of the A section, followed by the link passage which takes the music into section B.

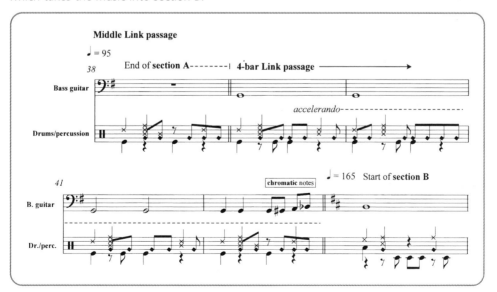

CD Track 70. You can now hear the finished piece, 'Jazzin' Around', in its entirety on CD track 70. Listen to it several times to familiarise yourself with the music and identify all the musical features discussed in this workshop. When you have done that, you can then go about finishing off your own jazz composition. Have fun!

Programme Note	'Jazzin' Around'	by Joe McGowan

Stimulus

I enjoy jazz music and improvising, and wanted to compose a piece of jazz music which, although based on improvisation, had a structure and a sense of direction – in a sense 'half-improvised and half-composed'.

Resources

Manuscript paper, MIDI keyboard and sequencer

Significant Decisions

I based 'Jazzin' Around' on an 8-bar chord progression which is varied throughout the piece and used as an ostinato 'backing' for the two solo instruments (piano and vibraphone) to improvise an extended melody over. I chose to build the melody from five main musical ideas which would be extended and developed by the solo instruments and bass guitar. The structure of the piece has two distinct sections, the first of which is in a moderate tempo (*moderato*) and the second a livelier *allegro* tempo; these are joined by a linking *accelerando* passage.

Use of technology

The piece was composed entirely with a MIDI keyboard and sequencer using a wide range of the sequencer's editing and composing facilities. I arranged it using a total of nine different sound patches before producing a final mix down in which I made fine adjustments to the volume of each track.

Use of improvisation

The piece is based on five melodic ideas, shared between the two solo parts and bass guitar, which I composed in an improvisatory style. Surrounding these main melodic ideas is music which is even more freely improvised in style.

Audio Recording Arrangements

At present only the MIDI file and a CD recording of this piece exist, but I plan to record a live performance in the studio at a later date.

Process

I began by composing the 8-bar chord progression which is used as an ostinato (varied in several ways) throughout the piece, to which I added sustained chords and a drum track. I then improvised in the key of G major until I had composed the first of five melodic ideas on which the piece is based. This improvising process was repeated at each stage of composition, often in different keys, with the piece gradually developing from the variation of these five melodic ideas and more freely improvised music.

GLOSSARY OF HIGHER MUSIC CONCEPTS

Acciaccatura – a note which is to be played as quickly as possible before the note it precedes. This is an *ornament*, written smaller than standard notes, with a line scored across it indicating that it has no time value and should be 'crushed in' very quickly.

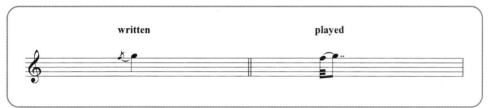

Added 6th chord – a chord which has the 6th note of the scale added to it – for example, the G major triad is made up of the notes G, B, D, and the sixth note of the G major scale is E, so the notes of the G6 chord are G, B, D, E. See *Chords and Cadences*, Chapter 1 section 5, page 16, and *Composing workshop 4*, page 97.

Air – a simple (often fairly slow) melody for voice or an instrument, but from about 1571 the term could also apply to lute music and ensemble songs; composers of this style include court lutenist John Dowland. The term 'air' was also used in late baroque suites and for instrumental pieces by Purcell, and by the mid seventeenth century in England it described a type of simple song. In traditional Scottish music an air is a slow tune that is either sung or played on an instrument such as the bagpipes or fiddle.

Anthem – a short choral work, whose text is taken from a moral or religious text in English, normally intended for performance in Church of England religious services. Early anthems (around 1550) consisted of four *contrapuntal* vocal parts which *imitated* each other, sometimes with *soloists* and organ *accompaniment*. In 1600 a development was the *verse style* or *verse anthem* (examples of which were written by English composers Byrd and Morley), where verses for solo voices and instrumental accompaniment (usually organ) alternated with choral passages. After 1661 a new style evolved with a *homophonic* texture and a succession of contrasting verses with occasional choruses. Purcell contributed to the development of this style, as well as to the *full anthem* and the newer *orchestral anthem*. Anthem composing continued in the eighteenth century with composers including Handel, and led to the development of the *American anthem*. The nineteenth century saw the Victorian revival of anthem composing, and the style even influenced twentieth century composers such as Britten, Walton and Vaughan Williams to write anthem-like pieces.

Antiphonal – a term which describes music or a method of performing where an ensemble is divided into two or more smaller groups which vary between playing together and alternating with each other.

Appoggiatura – a slightly discordant note on a strong beat which resolves, normally by moving one step upwards or (less often) downwards, onto the following note on the weaker beat. This is an *ornament* which is often written either as a standard note or as a small grace note.

Aria – a term used from the sixteenth century onwards to describe a song, but which came to be specifically associated with a song from an opera or oratorio. Earlier arias normally had a *continuo* accompaniment and instrumental *ritornellos* (repeated passages) between the sung verses, and by about 1680 were in the form ABB or ABA (the latter being the popular *Da Capo Aria* – see entry on page 124). In the eighteenth century the proportions changed, however, and much longer A sections were written along with shorter B sections which had a contrasting *tempo* and *metre*. Rondo form (ABACA) was also introduced, but arias in *comic operas* could have a much looser structure.

Augmentation – where a passage of music is repeated in longer note values than when it was first played.

Augmented chord – a triad made up of major third intervals – for example, the notes of the G augmented chord (G aug) are G, B, D♯. See *Chords and Cadences*, Chapter 1 section 5, page 16, and *Composing workshop 4*, page 95.

Ballet – Beginning as a dance form of Italian origin and later established in the sixteenth century at the French court, a ballet is now a story or drama that is portrayed through dance and music. Each dancer represents a character on stage with sets and scenery, accompanied throughout by music which is normally played by an orchestra positioned immediately in front of and below the stage in the 'pit' (as with an opera). The music for ballets is composed first, based on the subject matter or story the ballet is about, and then choreographed (where the dance moves are worked out using the music as a guide). Although normally consisting only of dance and music, ballet has sometimes also used singing – for example, Prokofiev's *Cinderella* (referred to as an *opera ballet*) and Ravel's *Daphnis et Chloe*.

Ballett – a type of vocal concert piece, popular in England and Italy around 1600, similar to the *madrigal* but more dance-like.

Basso Continuo – a term, sometimes abbreviated to 'continuo', for the instrument or instruments responsible for establishing the harmony in a piece of (mainly) baroque music. The continuo can consist of a single instrument such as *organ* (often used for sacred music), *harpsichord* (for smaller ensembles), *lute*, or, where a more *contrapuntal* texture is required in the bass part, a *cello*, *bassoon* or *bass viol* (see entry for *bass viol* under *consort*). More than one instrument could be used for the continuo, especially in larger-scale works, and in a late baroque concerto different continuo instruments would be used for the *ripieno* and *concertino* sections of the orchestra (see entries for *ripieno* and *concertino*). As the main role of the continuo was to support the melody by providing harmony and a bass line, it was gradually replaced in the classical period when composers wrote all the required harmony notes into the music itself, but the continuo continued to play a role in certain compositions.

Bridge – a passage which links two main sections of music together. For example, in a pop song the bridge might link a verse to the chorus, and in sonata form the bridge passage is used to link themes together in the exposition – which involves a key modulation. (See also entry for *Sonata form*.)

Cantata – since first appearing in the seventeenth century, the word 'cantata' has been used to describe various kinds of religious and non-religious music, but is mainly associated with a work, most popular in the baroque period, consisting of two or three *Da Capo arias* for solo voice and *continuo* with a *recitative* between each aria. In later periods all kinds of texts were used in cantata composition, with *chorus* and *orchestra* also incorporated into the form. Cantata composers include Alessandro Scarlatti, J S Bach, Telemann and Beethoven.

Chaconne/Passacaglia – although beginning as two distinct forms, in the art music of the baroque period there is little or no noticeable difference between the chaconne and the passacaglia: both are dances based on *variation* form, often associated with the use of a *ground bass*. Composers who wrote these works include Monteverdi, Lully, Bach and Purcell.

Chant – dating from as far back as the fourth century, the chant began as a form of slow singing used in religious and pagan ceremonies, long before any musical notation system had been devised. It developed and diversified over the centuries, and by medieval times 'plainchant' or 'plainsong' (a *monophonic unison* chant in Latin) was used in the Christian church. From this came the 'Gregorian chant', used in the Roman Catholic mass, consisting of a single vocal line with a free rhythm which followed the syllables of the Latin text – and therefore often had an irregular *metre* (by this stage chants were being written down using an early system which was quite unlike modern notation). This type of chant had three styles: *syllabic* (where each syllable is sung to a single, separate note), *neumatic* (where between two and twelve notes accompany a single syllable), and *melismatic* (where single syllables might be sung to many different notes). Later, the *Anglican chant*, a harmonised religious melody used for psalm-singing, was used in the Church of England.

Chorale – originally a hymn tune sung by the congregation of the German Lutheran church. The music and texts of the first chorales were frequently taken from earlier hymns and even non-religious songs. After 1600, however, new texts were normally written for four-part chorales which were based on an existing melody with three uncomplicated accompaniment parts. Chorale melodies themselves came to be used frequently as the basis for other pieces of music, and the chorale generally developed as a form, resulting in diverse styles such as the *chorale concerto* (a large sacred vocal work involving two or more vocal and instrumental choirs); the *chorale cantata* (a setting of a chorale text, or part of the text, in a cantata); the *chorale motet* (a vocal work, normally with instrumental doubling, where the chorale was used as the *cantus firmus*); the *chorale partita* or *chorale variations* (a set of variations based on the melody of a chorale); the *chorale fugue* (an organ fugue based on a chorale melody); the *chorale prelude* (a short work, normally for organ, based on a chorale, frequently used as an introduction or prelude to congregational singing in church); and the *chorale fantasia* (an organ piece based on a chorale but longer than a *chorale prelude*). Many of the finest chorales were written by J S Bach.

Chorale prelude – see entry for *Chorale*.

Chorus – a group of singers performing together, often divided into parts for different voice ranges (such as 'Soprano', 'Alto', 'Tenor' and 'Bass' – SATB) with more than one singer to each part. As well as functioning independently to perform choral music, choruses are found in works such as *oratorios*, *operas*, *cantatas*, *masses* and later *symphonies* – for example Beethoven's 9th Symphony (the 'Choral'), which was the first symphony to include a chorus, and Mahler's 8th Symphony (the 'Symphony of a Thousand'). *Chorus* is also a term given to the catchy part (refrain) of a modern song (such as a pop song or a folk song) which is repeated several times in the course of that song.

Coloratura – a term used, especially in vocal music, to describe sections decorated with florid, elaborate passages of notes or ornamentation. The technique requires considerable skill of the singer (normally a soprano); good examples can be found in some of Mozart's operas.

Concertino – The solo group in a baroque concerto or 'concerto grosso'. Later, the term could also mean a small-scale concerto.

Concerto grosso – a kind of baroque concerto comprising a concertino (small group of instruments) and the concerto grosso (main group of instruments). The purpose of having two groups was mainly so that they could provide contrast with each other.

Consonance – when musical notes sounding together are harmonious or 'pleasing' to the ear – for example, intervals of a third, fourth, fifth and an octave are consonant.

Consort – an old English term (which is derived from the Italian word 'concerto') for a small group of musicians. It is mainly in reference to sixteenth and seventeenth century music. The term can apply to groups of voices (with or without instruments), instrumental groups, and sometimes even to the music itself, but usually meant groups who played different kinds of musical instruments such as flute, lute, viol, bandora or cittern. (*Viols* were bowed string instruments of varying sizes with frets; smaller versions such as the treble viol (resembling a violin) would be played vertically on the lap, while the larger bass viol was played, like a cello, between the performer's legs. The *bandora* was a plucked string bass instrument with six or seven metal strings. The *cittern* was a wire string instrument which was plucked using a plectrum.) Composers of consort music include Purcell, Byrd and Morley.

Countersubject – see entry for *Fugue*.

Da Capo aria – an aria in *ternary form* (ABA) where the instruction '*Da Capo*' (go back to the beginning) is given at the end of the B section, as opposed to the A section being written out again.

Diminished chord – a triad made up of minor third intervals; for example, the notes of a G diminished chord are G, B♭, D♭.

Diminished 7th chord – a diminished chord (a triad made up of minor third intervals) with a diminished 7th interval (from the root note) added on top – for example, the notes of the G diminished chord are G, B♭, D♭, and with the added diminished 7th interval the notes are G, B♭, D♭, F♭ (G dim 7). See *Chords and Cadences*, Chapter 1 section 5, page 16, and *Composing workshop 4*, page 99.

Diminution – where a passage of music is repeated in shorter note values than when it was first played.

Dissonance – when musical notes sounding together are not harmonious, creating a discord or even a jarring and unpleasant sound – for example, intervals such as minor seconds, sixths and sevenths. Dissonance is effective in creating tension, drama, unrest, even horror!

Dominant 7th chord – the dominant chord (chord V) with a minor 7th interval (from the root note) added on top – for example, in the key of C major the dominant chord (chord V) is G major, which becomes G dominant 7th (G7) when the minor 7th interval is added (the chord notes now being G, B, D, F). See *Chords and Cadences*, Chapter 1 section 5, page 16, and *Composing workshop 4*, page 98.

Episode – can mean either a secondary section in a piece of music (such as one of the contrasting episodes in a *rondo*) or any passage in a *fugue* where the *subject* (main thematic material) is not played.

Exposition – the opening section in both *sonata* and *fugue* forms (see entries for *sonata* and *fugue*).

French overture – see entry for *Overture*.

Fugue – a musical structure/form, usually instrumental and in three or four parts, where each part (or 'voice' as they are often called) imitates the other successively, creating a *contrapuntal* texture. The main opening theme in a fugue (called the *subject*) is first played in the tonic key, and this is then imitated by another part (called the *answer*) normally in the dominant key. This alternating pattern is repeated throughout the fugue at different *octaves*. (A 'real' answer is one which is a precise note-for-note *transposition* of the *subject*, but sometimes this isn't desirable – where a 'real' answer would create *dissonance* with another part, for example – and certain intervals are altered to fit with the rest of the music. This is known as a 'tonal' answer.) When the *answer* is being played, the first voice will play a new main theme called the *countersubject* which is also followed by an *answer*. In between this overlapping texture of subject and answer phrases are sections of music called *episodes*. However, the pattern doesn't have to be so strict, and although this is the basic formula, many composers (notably J S Bach) varied the plan by adding original touches and variations to the general structure.

Galliard – A lively instrumental court dance (although it became a slower piece in its later style) in triple metre (three beats per bar), dating back to at least the fifteenth century. Normally played after a *pavan* to which it is thematically related, the galliard often uses a simple *homophonic* style (with the main tune in the upper part) and *hemiola*. Famous examples of the galliard can be found in the lute music of English composers John Dowland and Robert Johnson.

Harmonic minor – a version of the minor scale where the 7th note is raised by a semitone when the scale is both *ascending* and *descending*. For example, the notes of the scale of A harmonic minor are (ascending) A B C D E F G♯ A, (descending) A G♯ F E D C B A.

Harmonics – the individual sounds which are usually part of a musical note, and which give it its particular tone quality. Different instruments produce different numbers and types of harmonics, even when playing the same note, and this contributes to an instrument's unique sound. Other types of harmonics can be produced on many instruments; these are 'extra' high-pitched notes of a particular sound quality, with a clarity and sustain that cannot be achieved in normal playing. These kinds of harmonics can be produced on wind instruments by altering lip pressure and (in the case of woodwind instruments) by opening a nodal hole in the instrument; string instruments can produce 'natural' harmonics by touching a string at specific points (frets in the case of a guitar) before playing the string, and 'artificial' harmonics by fingering a note (as in normal playing) and touching/plucking the string either a fourth or an octave higher (depending on the instrument).

Hemiola – a rhythmic effect created by articulating two bars of music in *triple metre* in such a way that they sound like three bars of music in *duple metre*, sometimes achieved by changing the time signature from 3/4 to 6/8. A popular device in *renaissance* music and used in different kinds of music ever since.

Heterophony – where the same melody is played by two different instruments, or a voice and instrument, but one varies or embellishes the melody. For example, in some ethnic music a vocal melody can be accompanied by an instrument playing a decorated version of the same melody.

Hymn tune – a *strophic* religious song used in Christian worship, normally sung by church congregations.

Interrupted cadence – a *cadence* where chord V (the dominant chord) is followed by chord VI (the submediant chord), to create a slightly unexpected change of direction (or a little surprise) in the harmony, since the 'expected' chord I (which would complete a V–I *perfect cadence*) is replaced by chord VI (a minor chord) and so has 'interrupted' the perfect cadence. (See *Chords and Cadences*, Chapter 1 section 5, page 16.)

Inversion – has three distinct meanings. (1) The notes of a chord are rearranged so that the root note is replaced by another note in the chord. For example, in the chord of C major the notes are C, E, and G, with C being the lowest (root) note. If we replace the C with the next highest note, E, we create a *first inversion* of the C chord. Making the G the lowest note will result in a *second inversion* of the C chord. A form of musical 'shorthand' indicates first and second inversion chords with the letters 'b' and 'c' respectively. For example, if C major is the tonic chord (I), and its first inversion is used, this would be represented as Ib, and the second inversion as Ic. So, a *second inversion* of the *dominant* chord (which in the key of C major is *G major*) would be written as Vc. See *Composing workshop 2*, page 54. (2) The term *inversion* also applies to the technique of repeating a passage of music as a mirror image of itself, resulting in the repeating passage moving in opposite directions (or contrary motion) to the first. (3) The word *inversion* is also used to describe the inversion of an interval. For example, the interval between C and E this is a *third*, and when this is *inverted* (E to C) it becomes a *sixth*.

Irregular metres – when the number of beats per bar in a piece of music (the time signature) change frequently, creating an irregular main beat – for example, 3/4 – 2/4 – 6/8.

Italian overture – see entry for *Overture*.

Jazz-funk – a fusion of jazz and funk music.

Late romantic – the last of the three periods of the romantic era, lasting from about 1890 to around 1910. The romantic era existed from approximately 1790 to 1910, the early period ending around 1850 and the middle period 1890. Late romantic composers include Mahler, Rakhmaninov and R Strauss.

Leitmotiv – a musical idea or theme which represents a particular thing, person or idea in a piece of music. The leitmotiv will return periodically at relevant points in the piece, perhaps to remind us subtly of the person/thing on which the leitmotiv is based. The device is mainly associated with the romantic period (although it appeared much earlier) and dramatic works such as opera – for example, *Tristan und Isolde, Das Rheingold* and *Die Walküre* by Richard Wagner.

Lied (plural: *Lieder*) – German word for a song, but it refers more particularly to an art song of the romantic era written by composers such as Schumann, Mendelssohn, Wagner and R Strauss. Despite this association with romantic music, the term *Lied* has been used since the fifteenth century, but classical composers (including Mozart and Beethoven) began to develop the style, and this practice was continued by romantic composers. The songs (*Lieder*) – which were often *strophic, ternary* in structure, and *accompanied* by piano – focused on poetry, drama, scene-setting and character in an expressive way that was typical of the romantic period. The piano accompaniment became more important as the romantic era progressed, and composers such as Brahms, Wolf, Liszt and Schubert (who was widely recognised as one of the finest lieder composers) wrote intricate piano music for their songs. The development of lieder continued into the twentieth century, even though the tradition of song with piano accompaniment was lessening, and Mahler (who also wrote lieder with orchestral accompaniment), Schoenberg and Berg all composed original lieder.

Madrigal – a *contrapuntal* piece for several voices, sometimes with independent instrumental accompaniment, which developed from the *motet* and the French *chanson.* The word *madrigal* was first used in the fourteenth century to refer to poetic as well as musical forms, but from about the mid sixteenth century a madrigal was typically a musical work based on a non-religious verse (although some sacred madrigals were written) which concerned love or other human emotions. Madrigals for three voices and instrumental accompaniment were popular, and in the late sixteenth century composers experimented with *word painting, chromaticism* and *rhythmic* and *harmonic contrast.* One such composer was Monteverdi, who introduced a continuo part to the madrigal, and whose bold musical inventiveness in general helped to pave the way for the innovations of the proceeding baroque period. Although beginning in Italy, the madrigal later became popular in England, and by the first part of the seventeenth century solo madrigals were also being composed.

Mass – a large-scale vocal work based mainly on the Roman Catholic High Mass (which was sung). The mass is divided into two parts: the *Ordinary*, which is the unchanging sections of the mass (the *Kyrie, Gloria, Credo, Sanctus Benedictus, Agnus Dei* and *Benedicamus Domino*), and the *Proper*, a musical setting (normally based on plainchant) of those parts of the mass which were varied depending on the occasion (the *Introit, Gradual, Alleluia, Offertory* and *Communion*). Dating from the seventh century, the mass underwent various transformations over the centuries which were partly influenced by musical developments. The *chants* used in the earliest masses became the melodic material for the early *organum* of the tenth century, and from this the use of *polyphony* entered the mass. By the mid fifteenth century the *cantus firmus* or *tenor* mass was firmly established, which often used melodies from non-religious *chansons* as a source for the tenor part around which original melodies were composed. This practice of weaving existing material with new music was common, and masses could be based on *chansons*, *motets* or *madrigals* written by late renaissance composers such as Palestrina and Morales. There were also *freely invented* masses, *canonic masses* and *paraphrase masses*, all of which used different kinds of musical techniques in their composition. Masses which used either choruses with instrumental doubling, or solo voices and independent instrumental accompaniment, influenced the development of the *cantata mass* which divided the various sections of the mass into several movements; this style was used by baroque composers, including J S Bach, whose *B minor mass* is the finest example. Haydn and Mozart's masses of the classical period show the influence of the symphony in their style, and later masses by Beethoven (the *Missa Solemnis* in C), Liszt, Bruckner and Stravinsky were written for concerts or special occasions rather than religious services.

Melodic minor – a version of the minor scale where the 6th and 7th notes are raised by a semitone when the scale is ascending, but lowered again by one semitone when the scale descends. For example, the notes of the scale of A melodic minor are: (ascending) A B C D E **F♯ G♯** A, (descending) A **G F** E D C B A.

Microtone – a musical interval where the distance between two notes is less than a semitone. Microtones occur in some kinds of ethnic music and have been used since the time of ancient Greece, but it was not until the end of the nineteenth century that they appeared in Western music, when various composers began experimenting with quarter tones. Specially tuned pianos and organs were used at first (although microtones can also be produced on string instruments such as the guitar by bending the strings), but with the later development of electronic music in the twentieth century the scope for producing microtonal music greatly increased. Composers such as Bloch, Ohana and Carrilo have written this type of music.

Mode – a type of scale used in early music (medieval and renaissance periods) before tonal music (music with a key) was developed – although modal music is still in use today, especially in folk, rock and some ethnic music. The seven basic modes are called *Ionian*, *Dorian*, *Phrygian*, *Lydian*, *Mixolydian*, *Aeolean* and *Locrian*, and in their simplest form correspond to the white-note scales on C, D, E, F, G, A and B respectively. For example, if you begin on the note D on a keyboard instrument and play only the successive *white* keys for an octave, this is the *Dorian* mode. Do the same on the note F and you will play the notes of the *Lydian* mode. The specific order of tones and semitones (no black keys are used) give each mode its unique sound. For further information, see *Composing Workshop 3*, page 71.

Mordent – an *ornament* consisting of a rapid playing of the written note followed by the note a step above and then the written note again. A mordent is indicated by the symbol ♦ .

Motet – a *polyphonic* vocal composition, often with two vocal parts and two instrumental parts, mainly religious (although non-religious motets exist), which was important from medieval times through to the eighteenth century and also influenced the development of other musical forms. Earlier motets were built upon an existing religious tenor voice part, the *cantus firmus*, over which up to three upper voices sang a faster melody; this style became popular around 1450, by which time it was common for motets to consist of between four and six individual parts. *Imitative counterpoint* and *polyphony* were used in the sixteenth century motet, and the baroque period saw the inclusion of instrumental parts doubling the voices as well as a continuo accompaniment. Voices with continuo (the '*vocal concerto*') became very popular, and by the mid baroque period the *orchestral motet* had developed, which was similar to the operatic forms of the time. The influence of the motet led to the appearance of the *aria*, the *chorale*, the eighteenth century *church cantata* and the *choral motet*, which was developed for weddings, funerals and special occasions – J S Bach's six motets are the finest examples of this form. Other motet composers include Palestrina, Mozart, Liszt and Brahms.

Musique concrète – a term first used in the late 1940s by electronic composers in Paris to describe 'concrete' sounds that are recorded (rather than being written down as musical notation that has to be performed later).

Nationalist – a term applied to music which in some way reflects aspects of the nationality of a country; this could be achieved through the use of folk melodies, traditional dance rhythms, and even the musical instruments associated with a particular country. Although composers of the seventeenth and eighteenth centuries sometimes used the folk melodies of their countries in their compositions, it wasn't until the mid-nineteenth century that Nationalism became a popular movement in music. Composers including Debussy (France), Sibelius (Finland), Holst (England), Musorgsky (Russia) and Wagner (Germany) all incorporated nationalist elements in some of their works.

Neo-classical – a term describing a twentieth-century style where some composers (for example, Stravinsky, Schoenberg and Prokofiev) wrote music in the earlier style of classical music.

Oratorio – a large work for orchestra (consisting of *ripieno* and *concertino* sections, each with its own *continuo*), *chorus* and soloists, based on a religious or moral text and normally set dramatically. In its earlier forms (around 1600–1650), scenery and costumes were also used (as in an opera), but these were discarded in later oratorios which were written for concert performance only. From the mid seventeenth century onwards the more developed oratorio was typically a work in two sections (which could last up to two hours in total) with many *Da Capo arias* and a few *choruses*. Famous oratorios come from the baroque and early classical periods, such as *Messiah* by Handel, and *The Creation* and *The Seasons* by Haydn, but later composers also wrote oratorios, including Liszt (*Christus*), Elgar (*The Dream of Gerontius*) and Walton (*Belshazzar's Feast*). Although normally a religious work, some non-religious oratorios were also written, such as *Semele* by Handel and *A Child of our Time* by twentieth century composer Michael Tippett.

Organised sound – a term relating to certain kinds of modern music which does not follow the conventions of pitch, harmony and rhythm normally associated with a piece of music. Such compositions may sound more like an arrangement or 'organisation' of sounds than music in the accepted sense.

Overture – the overture is a short orchestral piece which normally introduces a much larger work, such as an opera or oratorio. The French overture in the *baroque* period was a two-movement work which normally began slowly in duple metre before moving into a faster triple metre (sometimes returning again to the slow speed before the end). The later Italian overture, or *sinfonia*, of the late seventeenth century was based on a three section *fast-slow-fast* structure in which the trumpet often had an important part. This structure continued into the classical period (and from this form the *symphony* evolved), but composers including Gluck and Mozart also began incorporating themes from the proceeding opera into the overture, and so linked the two works together more closely. By the end of the eighteenth century the overture normally consisted of a slow beginning followed by a fast section in basic *sonata* form with no repeats. Around the mid nineteenth century the *concert overture* existed: one-movement orchestral works written as pieces in their own right, such as Mendelssohn's *The Hebrides* – a piece inspired by the Scottish Hebridean Islands. As well as being descriptive, these orchestral overtures could also be inspired by events or literary subjects (stories) – for example *King Lear* by Berlioz, which is based on the play by Shakespeare.

Passion – a piece which portrays the story of the crucifixion of Jesus Christ as told in the four biblical gospels. Often set dramatically with individual singers playing the roles of the important biblical characters, the passion was intended to be sung in churches in the lead-up to Easter. It began in the thirteenth century as a work for three singers and chorus, but different forms of the passion developed over time (the largest being for orchestra, chorus and soloists), and innovations such as the inclusion of musical instruments, narrators, hymns, verses and soloists led to the appearance of the *motet passion*, *responsorial passion* (also known as the *choral passion* or *dramatic passion*), *oratorio passion* (of which J S Bach's *St John Passion* and *St Matthew Passion* are the finest examples), *passion meditation* and *passion oratorio*, as well as various mixtures or 'hybrids' of these. Modern performances of passions are associated more with concert halls than churches.

Pavan – A slow and stately instrumental court dance (dating from at least the sixteenth century), normally in duple metre (two beats per bar), which is followed by a faster dance (or dances) in triple metre, particularly the *galliard*. A famous example from the romantic era is the *Pavan pour une Infante défunte* (Pavan for a dead Infanta – a Spanish princess) by Ravel.

Plagal cadence – a *cadence* where chord IV (the subdominant chord) is followed by chord I (the tonic chord). Sometimes called an 'Amen' cadence because it is often used at the end of hymns on the word 'Amen'. (See *Chords and Cadences*, Chapter 1 section 5, page 16.)

Plainchant (or Plainsong) – a religious *monophonic unison* chant sung in Latin, which dates back to the early Christian church. Sometimes also referred to as 'Gregorian chant'.

Polytonality – when more than two different keys are used *at the same time* in a piece of music.

Prelude – a term, dating from the fifteenth century, for an instrumental piece or movement which begins ('precedes') a larger work or a group of pieces – for example, the first piece in a suite. In the baroque period a prelude was normally followed by a *fugue* or a *suite* of pieces; such preludes were often written in the French prelude style (and were commonly followed by a suite of French dances), which had an element of *improvisation*. J S Bach wrote a number of French suites, and his famous forty-eight preludes and fugues are among the finest examples of the prelude and fugue combination (which was mainly a German style). Few preludes were written in the classical period, but in the nineteenth century some composers (such as Brahms, Liszt and Mendelssohn) wrote preludes and fugues, having been influenced by the music of J S Bach. More typical in the romantic period was the independent piano prelude which existed as a piece in its own right, and these were written by composers including Chopin, Debussy and Rakhmaninov.

Real Answer – see entry for *fugue*.

Recitative – a form of speech-singing (half-spoken, half-sung) where the performer has some freedom with the rhythm (which closely follows the natural rhythm of speech); sometimes this freedom also extends to the notes and how they are sung. Used in works such as *opera* and *oratorio* to lead into a song or as a means of linking *arias*, but also as a device to inform the audience of a plot development and so move the drama along (this could be a dialogue between two characters, for example). Two main kinds of recitative are: *accompanied recitative*, which is accompanied by instruments, continuo or orchestra, and *dry recitative*, which is almost entirely unaccompanied, except for the occasional appearance of an instrument such as a harpsichord to punctuate certain of the speaker's words.

Renaissance – a term, meaning 'rebirth' (of ancient Greek and Roman values), given to the period between the medieval and baroque periods (about 1430 to 1600). Music of the renaissance includes *chansons, masses, motets* and *madrigals*, as well as instrumental *consort* music. A characteristic style of the period is *imitative counterpoint* (or *imitative polyphony*) in four or more parts, in compositions written by composers such as Palestrina and Byrd. Two very popular instruments of the time were the recorder and the lute.

Retrograde – where a passage of notes is played backwards. The technique was first used in medieval and renaissance music, but is also important in twelve-note (or *note row*) music such as Schoenberg's where twelve-note rows can be used in both *retrograde* and *retrograde inversion* (see entry for *Inversion*).

Ripieno – the *tutti* ('everyone' or '*concerto grosso*') section, as distinct from the solo group (or '*concertino*'), of a baroque orchestra, especially in concertos.

Ritornello – a term used mainly in baroque music to describe a brief passage which keeps recurring (normally alternating with the soloist), mainly in the instrumental *tutti* ('everyone') sections of a baroque *concerto* or *aria*.

Scherzo (a 'joke') – a playful, light hearted piece in a quick tempo. In early seventeenth century Italian music the term was first used for light *madrigals*, but from about 1650 to 1750 not many scherzos (or scherzi) were written, and these were instrumental pieces. In classical music the scherzo dates from Haydn's quartets, but Beethoven established the *scherzo and trio* as an alternative to the *minuet* in *sonatas, symphonies* and *chamber music*. Later, the scherzo became an independent movement, as exemplified in Chopin's four piano *Scherzi*, or Brahms's *Scherzo* opus 4.

Serial – a composing method where musical elements (note pitches, rhythm, etc.) are set into an order or a fixed 'series'. This normally involves setting the notes and pitches in a specific way, such as arranging the twelve notes of the *chromatic scale* into a particular order to create a series or 'row' on which an entire piece of music will be structured. This note-row or series can be altered using techniques such as *retrograde*, *inversion*, *retrograde inversion*, and by transposing the series up or down by any interval. Notes may be repeated (but the order of the notes in the series is not normally altered) and chords can also be used. Serialism began with Schoenberg in the 1920s and was adopted by his pupils Webern and Berg and later (after 1945) by Boulez, Stockhausen and Stravinsky, who expanded and developed the technique by setting elements such as note duration, attack (accents, sforzando, etc.) and dynamics into a fixed series.

Sonata – a piece of instrumental music, normally in a number of movements, for a small ensemble or a soloist. The term was originally used from the late sixteenth century to describe something which was played rather than sung.

Sonata Form – the most important structure for instrumental music from the classical period to the twentieth century. The form consists of three main sections. (1) The first section, the *exposition*, 'exposes' the main musical material, which consists of a number of *themes* divided into the *first subject* (in the *tonic* key) and the *second subject* (normally in either the *dominant* or *relative* key), separated by a *transition* or *bridge* passage, and concluded by a *codetta* (brief Coda). (2) The second section, the *development*, 'develops' the material of the *exposition* by *repeating* it with *variation* and in several different keys, ending in the *tonic* key in preparation for the next section. (3) The final section, the *recapitulation*, 'recaps' the themes used in the *exposition* (perhaps with some key changes), normally in the same order, but with the *second subject* now in the *tonic* key. Sometimes an *Introduction* and a *Coda* are added to this basic sonata structure.

Song cycle – a group of songs where each song is complete in itself, but linked together by a common aspect such as a narrative (story) or theme. Song cycles, which evolved in the nineteenth century, were written by composers including Debussy, Schubert, Fauré, Schumann and Mahler.

Sprechgesang – 'Speech song': a vocal technique which is halfway between singing and speech; used by twentieth-century composers including Schoenberg and Berg.

Stretto – the term can mean either (1) the technique of introducing (in quick succession) two or more entries of the *subject* (main theme) in a *fugue*, or (2) a change to a faster *tempo* in a climactic or dramatic point in a piece of music – such as the finale of an opera.

Subject – see entry for *Fugue*.

Suite – a collection of pieces intended to be played in succession in a single performance to form a large instrumental work. The individual pieces were commonly a collection of dances in the same key but with a different *style*/character, *tempo* and *metre*. In the baroque period the common dances were the French *Bourrée* (a lively dance in duple metre), *Allemande* (a moderate-tempo dance normally in quadruple metre), *Courante* (a moderate-tempo dance, usually in triple metre, with a contrapuntal texture), *Sarabande* (a slow dance normally in triple metre), *Minuet* (a dance in moderate triple metre) and *Gigue* (a lively dance in moderate or fast tempo and usually in 3/4, 6/8 or 9/8 time). The popularity of suites faded in the classical period when other instrumental forms such as the *symphony*, *sonata* and *concerto* developed, but Mozart and later composers including Ravel, Strauss, Debussy and Schoenberg all wrote suites. The term 'suite' in the nineteenth and twentieth centuries was also used for a collection of movements from a large-scale work such as an opera or ballet, and for a group of pieces or movements linked by a single theme (a nationalist theme, for example) or a descriptive programme, such as *The Planets* by Holst.

Symphonic/tone poem – a form of orchestral music based specifically on a story, programme, poem or event which the music alone portrays or 'narrates'. The form can be seen to have begun evolving in certain of Beethoven's overtures (the *Egmont Overture,* for example) which describe actual events, and in those of Mendelssohn and Berlioz. Composers of the symphonic poem include Liszt (who introduced the term), Tchaikovsky (*Romeo and Juliet*), Saint-Saëns (*Danse macabre*), Richard Strauss (*Also sprach Zarathustra*) and Sibelius (*The Swan of Tuonela*). Nationalistic ideas were also used in the symphonic poems of Smetana, Dvorak, Musorgsky and Borodin. The main difference between a symphony and a symphonic poem is that a symphonic poem portrays something non-musical, such as a piece of literature.

Three against two – where the notes of a *triplet* play at the same time as two notes which 'add up' to the same value – for example, three crotchet triplet notes might play against two crotchet beats.

Tierce de Picardie – a technique commonly used in the renaissance and baroque periods where a piece of music in a minor key ends on the tonic major chord – for example, a piece in A minor would finish with an A major chord.

Time change – when the time signature suddenly changes in a piece of music – for example, 4/4 – 3/4.

Tonal Answer – see entry for *fugue*.

Tonal sequence – a musical sequence (where a figure or a passage is repeated at different pitches) which is not an exact transposition of the original passage but a version in which certain notes are altered in order to 'fit' harmonically with other parts of the piece.

Tone row (or note row) – the order of the notes (selected by the composer) in a piece of twelve-note music – that is, music which uses the twelve notes (all the semitones) in an octave to create *atonal* compositions.

Transition – a passage, often involving a key modulation, which leads one main section of a piece of music into another (such as the *bridge passage* joining the first and second subjects together in *sonata* form).

Tritone ('three tones') – a musical interval resulting from three whole tones. For example, the notes G–A–B–C♯ form three whole tone intervals (the notes are a tone apart); the interval between the first and last notes, G–C♯, is an augmented fourth, and is known as a tritone. Tritones are exactly half an octave.

Turn – an *ornament* consisting of four notes, indicated by the symbol ∾ above a single note. The ornament begins on (1) the note above the written note, followed by (2) the written note, then (3) the note below, and finally (4) the written note once again. The rhythm of the turn depends on the value of the original written note, but normally involves four notes of equal time value. For example, a turn on a crotchet (quarter note) beat would be played as four semiquaver (sixteenth) notes.

CONCEPTS FROM PREVIOUS GRADES

Below is a list of concepts covered in previous grades which you also need to know. Knowledge of these concepts will be assumed at Higher grade, and therefore it is essential that you understand them. For definitions and further information on these concepts see some of the websites listed on page 6, and also *How To Pass Standard Grade Music*, published by Hodder Gibson. (**Note**: Access 3, Intermediate 1 and Intermediate 2 equate closely to Foundation, General and Credit levels respectively, at Standard Grade.)

ACCESS 3		
MELODY	**HARMONY**	**RHYTHM**
Ascending melody	Chord	Faster, slower
Descending melody	Chord change	Pause
Stepwise melody	Discord	Repetition
Leaping melody		Beat/pulse
Repetition		Simple time: 2, 3 and 4
Sequence		beats in the bar
Broken chord		On the beat
Phrase		Off the beat
Question and Answer		Accented
		Drum fill
		Pattern
		Scotch snap

STRUCTURE	**TIMBRE**	**STYLE/FORM**
Solo	Louder, Softer	Baroque
Ensemble	Sound, Silence	Scottish
Harmony	Sustained	March
Single line	Staccato, Legato	Strathspey
Unison/octave	Striking, Bowing, Blowing,	Reel
Ostinato/riff	Plucking, Strumming,	Waltz
Accompanied	Slapping	Rock
Unaccompanied	Orchestra: Woodwind,	Jazz
Repetition	Brass, Strings, Percussion	Pop
Contrast	Bands: Brass, Pipe, Rock, Steel,	Latin-American
Section	Wind/Military, Scottish Dance	
Round	Groups: folk, pop, jazz	
	Instruments: acoustic guitar,	
	electric guitars, drum kit,	
	keyboard, piano, organ,	
	synthesizer, pipes, accordion,	
	fiddle	
	Voice, vocal, choral, lead	
	vocals, backing vocals	

INTERMEDIATE 1		
MELODY	**HARMONY**	**RHYTHM**
Semitone	Tonality: major and minor	Down beat
Tone	Change of key	Up beat
Theme	Chord progressions using	Anacrusis
Variation	chords I, IV and V in major	Speed change:
Imitation	keys	rallentando, rubato,
Ornament	Drone	accelerando
Scales: pentatonic, major,	Vamp	Compound time
minor, chromatic		Syncopation
Scat singing		

STRUCTURE	TIMBRE	STYLE/FORM
Chords	Individual instruments:	Fanfare
Arpeggio	orchestra, folk, Scottish,	Opera
Cluster	keyboard, recorders,	Concerto
Walking bass	pan pipes	Symphony
Descant	Voices: Soprano, Alto, Tenor,	Romantic
Contrary motion	Bass (SATB)	Musical
Binary AB	Chamber music	Blues
Ternary ABA, AABA	Ceilidh band	Ragtime
Canon	Latin percussion ensemble	Swing
Rondo	Gamelan	Gaelic psalms
Minuet and Trio	Ghanaian drum ensemble	Bothy ballad
Theme and Variations	Electronic drums	Scots ballad
Middle 8	Effects: bending, distortion,	Slow air
Programme	rolls, delay, reverb	Mouth music
	Crescendo	Waulking song
	Diminuendo	Indonesian gamelan
		Ghanaian
		Jig
		Samba
		Salsa
		Improvisation

INTERMEDIATE 2		
MELODY	**HARMONY**	**RHYTHM**
Tonal	Passing note	Groupings in simple
Atonal	Interval	and compound time
Relative major	Suspension	Dotted rhythms
Relative minor	Consonance	Cross rhythms
Modulating	Dissonance	Triplets
Trill	Tierce de Picardie	
Grace note	Perfect cadence	
Interval	Imperfect cadence	
Syllabic word setting	Chord progressions using	
Melismatic word	chords I, IV, V and VI in	
setting	major and minor keys	
Blues scale	Modulation	
Whole-tone scale	Modulation to relative	
Word painting	minor	

STRUCTURE	**TIMBRE**	**STYLE/FORM**
Ground bass	Voices: Mezzo-Soprano,	Hymn tune
Alberti bass	Countertenor, Baritone	Aria
Pedal	Glissando	Passion
Inverted pedal	Muted/con sordino	Chorale
Homophony	Double stopping	Oratorio
Polyphony	Flutter tonguing	Cantata
Countermelody	Arco	Recitative
Contrapuntal	Col legno	Classical
Strophic	Pizzicato	Scherzo
Obbligato	Vibrato	Impressionist
Through-composed	Tremolando/tremolo	Chorus
Cadenza	A cappella	Minimalist
Coda	Register	Dixieland
	12-string guitar	Boogie-woogie
	Slide guitar	Country
	Fretless bass guitar	Soul
	Sitar	Indian
	Tabla	Aleatoric
		Pibroch

ANSWERS TO LISTENING EXERCISES IN CHAPTERS 1 AND 2

Chapter 1: Revising Higher Music Concepts

Section 1: Early music

CD track 1 / Question 1

Column One

☑ Madrigal

Column Two

☑ Syncopation

CD track 2 / Question 2

Column One

☑ Chant

Column Two

☑ Voices in unison

CD track 3 / Question 3

Column One

☑ Galliard

Column Two

☑ Triple metre

CD track 4 / Question 4

Column One

☑ Motet

Column Two

☑ Melismatic

CD track 5 / Question 5

Column One

☑ Mass

Column Two

☑ Polyphonic

Answers continued

Section 2: Baroque music

CD track 6 / Question 6

- ☑ Concerto grosso
- ☑ Imitation
- ☑ Ripieno

CD track 7 / Question 7

- ☑ Oratorio
- ☑ Homophonic SATB
- ☑ Sequence

CD track 8 / Question 8

- ☑ Cantata
- ☑ Syllabic
- ☑ Pedal

CD track 9 / Question 9

- ☑ Fugue
- ☑ Real answer
- ☑ Legato

Section 3: Classical and romantic music

CD track 10 / Question 10

- ☑ Lied
- ☑ Triplets
- ☑ Harmonic minor
- ☑ Staccato

CD track 11 / Question 11

- ☑ Coloratura
- ☑ Appoggiatura
- ☑ Aria
- ☑ Opera

Answers *continued*

CD track 12 / Question 12

- ☑ Romantic
- ☑ Tremolando/tremolo
- ☑ Three against two
- ☑ Symphony

CD track 13 / Question 13

- ☑ Acciaccatura
- ☑ Muted trumpets
- ☑ Late romantic
- ☑ Ritardando (*rit.*)

Section 4: Modern music

CD track 14 / Question 14

- ☑ Trill
- ☑ Double stopping
- ☑ Harmonics
- ☑ Glissando

CD track 15 / Question 15

- ☑ Serial
- ☑ Pizzicato
- ☑ Cross rhythms
- ☑ Glissando

CD track 16 / Question 16.

- ☑ Modulation
- ☑ Sequence
- ☑ Reverb
- ☑ Bridge

CD track 17 / Question 17

- ☑ Pitched percussion
- ☑ Irregular metres
- ☑ Unpitched percussion
- ☑ Tone row

Answers *continued*

Section 5: Chords and cadences

CD track 18 / Question 18

☑ Interrupted cadence

CD track 19 / Question 19

☑ Plagal cadence

CD track 20 / Question 20

☑ Imperfect cadence

CD track 21 / Question 21

☑ Perfect cadence

CD track 22 / Question 22

☑ Augmented chord

CD track 23 / Question 23

☑ Diminished 7th chord

CD track 24 / Question 24

☑ Added 6th chord

CD track 25 / Question 25

☑ Dominant 7th chord

CD track 26 / Question 26

☑ Major 7th chord

Section 6: Musical Literacy

CD track 27
Musical Literacy Exercise 1

(a) **4**
    4

(b) See notation at top of p.141

(c) See notation at top of p.141

(d) **Pizzicato**

(e) **Phrase lines**

(f) **Gradually quieter** (or *decrescendo* or *diminuendo*)

Answers *continued*

CD track 28
Musical Literacy Exercise 2

(a) **Tie**

(b)

(c) See notation below

(d) Bar 10 (see notation below)

(e) See notation below

(f) **Sequence** or **Modulation**

CD track 29
Musical Literacy Exercise 3

(a) **3**
   4

(b) *Sforzando* (suddenly loud)

Answers *continued*

(c) See notation below

(d)

(e) See notation below

(f) **First time and second time bars**

(g) **Natural**

Chapter 2: Sample Listening Test Question Paper

CD track 30
Question 1(a)

☑ Rubato

☑ Tremolando/tremolo

☑ Broken chords

☑ Slurs

Question 1(b)

(i) **Minor**

(ii) ☑ Duet

CD track 31
Question 2

Answers continued

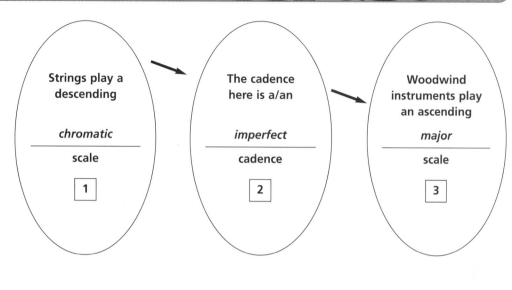

Strings play a descending

chromatic

scale

1

→ The cadence here is a/an

imperfect

cadence

2

→ Woodwind instruments play an ascending

major

scale

3

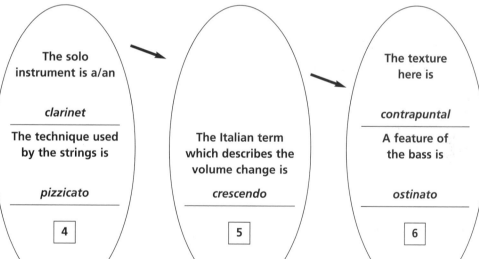

The solo instrument is a/an

clarinet

The technique used by the strings is

pizzicato

4

→ The Italian term which describes the volume change is

crescendo

5

→ The texture here is

contrapuntal

A feature of the bass is

ostinato

6

CD track 32
Question 3

☑ Renaissance

☑ Consort

☑ Tierce de Picardie

☑ Imitative polyphony

Answers *continued*

CD track 33
Question 4 (a)

(i) **Acciaccatura**

(ii) **6**
     8

(iii) **First and second**

(iv) **A major**

(v)

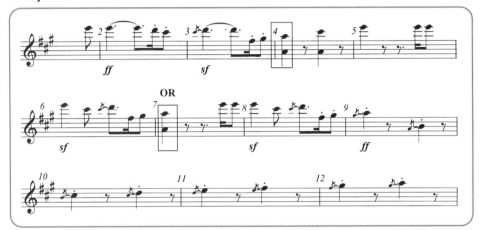

(vi) **Crescendo** (gradually louder)

(vii) **Staccato**

Question 4 (b)

Column 1

☑ Classical

Column 2

☑ Symphony

CD track 34
Question 5 (a)

☑ Baroque

☑ Basso continuo

☑ Concerto

Question 5 (b)

(i) **Oboe**

(ii) ☑ Sequence   ☑ Staccato

Answers *continued*

CD Track 35
Question 6

The excerpt begins with the vocal line 'Oh I got my ticket ready and the time is gettin' short 'cos we're leavin' today…' The type (range) of voice singing this line is a <u>soprano</u>*. The solo voice is soon accompanied by a* <u>chorus</u> *of singers. Shortly after this, the composer uses certain instruments/musical devices to suggest a moving train; list at least three of these:*

<u>string ostinato; xylophone; shaker</u> (unpitched percussion instrument)<u>;</u>
<u>trumpet; snare/side drum; musical rhythm imitates the mechanical</u>
<u>rhythm of a steam train</u>.

Music which describes something in this way is called <u>programmatic</u> *(or* <u>programme music</u>*). A section then begins with the singers accompanied by solo piano. A word to describe the style of the singing here is* <u>syllabic</u> *(or* <u>homophonic</u>*), and a feature of the piano accompaniment is* <u>ostinato</u>*. When the piano stops playing the singers begin an unaccompanied section; this kind of unaccompanied singing is known as* <u>A cappella</u>*, and the structure here is* <u>polyphonic</u>*. From here to the end of the excerpt the voices sing the same lyrics but not in unison; the higher-pitched voices sing the melody in quicker note values than those at the lower pitch – this is known as* <u>diminution</u>*, whereas the lower voices do the opposite and sing the notes in longer note values, which is known as* <u>augmentation</u>*.*
Finally, what style or styles of music (i.e. folk, rock, blues, etc.) do you think had the greatest influence on the composition of this piece? <u>Jazz and/or Gospel</u>.

CD Tracks 36 and 37.
Question 7

[GRID 2]: Final answer

CONCEPTS	EXCERPT 1	EXCERPT 2	COMMON TO BOTH EXCERPTS
MELODIC Trill			
Imitation	✔		
Atonal			
Modal			
Microtone			
HARMONIC Suspension			
Modulation			✔
Polytonality			
Whole-tone scale			
Alberti bass			
STRUCTURAL Canon			
Ostinato		✔	
Triple metre		✔	
Aria			✔
Polyphonic			
STYLES/FORMS Baroque			
Classical	✔		
Late romantic		✔	
Opera			✔
Oratorio			
	2 marks	3 marks	3 marks

CD TRACK LIST

CD track	Title	Composer (Performers)	Recording Co.	Page
1	Leggiadre ninfe	P. de Monte (The Amaryllis Consort)	(IMP Red Label Innovative Music Productions) PCD 822	9
2	Claris Coniubila	Traditional	Music Collection International MCCD 130	9
3	Galliard	Anonymous (Joe McGowan)	Hodder Gibson	9
4	Exsultate Deo	Palestrina (Christ Church Cathedral Choir; director, Stephen Darlington)	Nimbus Records Limited NI 5100	10
5	Kyrie (Mass for Pentecost)	Palestrina (Christ Church Cathedral Choir; director, Stephen Darlington)	Nimbus Records Limited NI 5100	10
6	Concerto no. 6 in F major	Arcangelo Corelli (The English Concert; Trevor Pinnock)	Polydor International 423 626-2	10
7	Chorus and Soli (The Creation Oratorio)	Joseph Haydn (The English Baroque Soloists; The Monteverdi Choir; Conductor John Eliot Gardiner)	Archiv Produktion 449 217-2	11
8	Recitative and Arioso: Ich stehe fertig und bereit	Johann Sebastian Bach (Thomas Quasthoff (bass-baritone); members of the RIAS-Kammerchor; chorus master: Daniel Reuss)	Deutsche Grammophon 477 532-6	11
9	Contrapunctus V (The Art of Fugue)	JS Bach (Karl Munchinger Stuttgarter Kammerorchester)	The Decca Record Company Limited, London 467 267-2	11
10	Ständchen	Franz Schubert (Peter Schreier (tenor); Andras Schiff (piano))	The Decca Record Company Limited, London 425 612-2	12

CD track	Title	Composer *(Performers)*	Recording Co.	Page
11	**Non mi dir, bell' idol mio,** from *Don Giovanni*	**W A Mozart** *(The Drottningholm Court Theatre Orchestra. Conductor: Arnold Ostman; Soprano: Arleen Augér)*	The Decca Record Company Limited, London **CD2 470 059-2**	13
12	**Bewegt, nicht zu schnell**, from Symphony no. 4	**Anton Bruckner** *(The Berlin Philharmonic Orchestra; Eugen Jochum)*	Deutsche Grammophon **449 718-2**	13
13	**Movement 2**, from Symphony no. 9	**Gustav Mahler** *(Chicago Symphony Orchestra (Sir Georg Solti))*	The Decca Record Company Limited, London **410 012-2**	13
14	**Lil Darlin**	**Martin Taylor**	P3 Music Ltd **P3MOO5**	14
15	**Dieses Bild Bezeugt**	**Arnold Schoenberg** *(The Royal Concertgebouw Orchestra; Pierre Boulez)*	Deutsche Grammophon **449 174-2**	14
16	**SOS**	**ABBA**	Polar Music International AB, A Universal Music Company **549 974-2**	15
17	**Movement IV: Rythmique,** from Notations I–IV (for orchestra)	**Pierre Boulez** *(Vienna Philharmonic Orchestra with Claudio Abbado)*	Deutsche Grammophon **429 260-2**	15
18–26	**Musical examples**	**Joe McGowan**	**Hodder Gibson**	17–19
27	**Andante quasi Allegretto**, from Symphony no. 4	**Anton Bruckner** *(The Berlin Philharmonic Orchestra; Eugen Jochum)*	Deutsche Grammophon **449 718-2**	20
28	**Bewegt, nicht zu schnell**, from Symphony no. 4	**Anton Bruckner** *(The Berlin Philharmonic Orchestra; Eugen Jochum)*	Deutsche Grammophon **449 718-2**	20
29	**Movement 3: Tempo di menuetto**, from Symphony no. 8	**Ludwig van Beethoven** *(The Vienna Philharmonic; Orchestra; Claudio Abbado)*	Deutsche Grammophon **423 364-2**	22
30	**Spanish Portrait**	**Joe McGowan and Cameron Angus**	Casa Tegoyo	23

CD track	Title	Composer *(Performers)*	Recording Co.	Page
31	**Movement 3: Scene aux champs**, from *Symphonie Fantastique*	**Hector Berlioz** *(Chicago Symphony Orchestra (Sir Georg Solti))*	The Decca Record Company Limited, London **417 705-2**	23
32	**Sio Esca Vivo**	**O.de Lassus** *(The Amaryllis Consort)*	IMP Red Label Innovative Music Productions **PCD 822**	24
33	**Movement 1: Poco sostenuto – vivace**, from Symphony no. 7	**Ludwig van Beethoven** *(The Vienna Philharmonic Orchestra; Claudio Abbado)*	Deutsche Grammophon **423 364-2**	25
34	**Allegro from Concerto in C major, RV 450**	**Vivaldi** *(Oboe: Douglas Boyd; the chamber orchestra of Europe)*	Deutsche Grammophon **435 873-2**	26
35	**Headin' for the Promis' Lan'** ('Oh, the train is at the station')	**George Gershwin** *(Cleveland Orchestra & Chorus. Conductor: Lorin Maazel)*	The Decca Record Company Limited, London **414 559-2**	26
36	**'Ce a caso madama'**, from *The Marriage of Figaro*	**W A Mozart** *(London Opera Chorus; London Philharmonic Orchestra; conductor: Sir Georg Solti)*	The Decca Record Company Limited, London **410 150-2**	27
37	**'Jak razem vsecko to Stevkovo vypinani schliplo'**, from *Jenufa*	**Leos Janacek** *(Wieslav Ochman; Petr Dvorsky; Vienna Philharmonic Orchestra; conductor: Charles Mackerras)*	The Decca Record Company Limited, London **414 483-2**	27
38	**Scarborough Fair**	**Traditional** *(Joe McGowan)*	Hodder Gibson	46
39–70	**Musical examples**	**Joe McGowan**	Hodder Gibson	55–119

149